Lord and Savior

A Savior to be Received From
A Lord to be Obeyed

Tom Peers

Lord and Savior

A Savior to be Received From
A Lord to be Obeyed

Ragamuffin Publishing Company - Portland, Maine

tompeers53@gmail.com

Lord and Savior/ Tom Peers. – 1st ed.

ISBN 10: 0-9970998-3-6
ISBN 13: 978-0-9970998-3-6

In this book I am using the American form of the word, "Savior," not the English form, "Saviour."

Man, mankind, he, him and *his* are used generically to mean all men and women...all of humankind.

Websites cited in endnotes were accessed at the time of writing and may not be active today.

I wrote this book primarily for myself.
You may find it helpful as well.

CHAPTER 1

Troubling Observations

Since accepting Christ in the summer of 1970, I have noticed something troubling, and that is how seriously (or more precisely, non-seriously) Christians take their relationship with Jesus Christ. This is not to say that I've expected them to read their bibles and pray three hours every day, or sell everything they own and move to the mission field, but it does mean that I've noticed the absence of something Scripture is very clear about in defining true Christ-followers...ongoing active commitment, that of "continuing."

John 8:31

So Jesus was saying to those Jews who had believed Him, "If you **continue** *in My word, then you are truly disciples of Mine." (NASB)*

A disciple is one who "continues," a convert is someone who doesn't. A convert says a one-time sinner's prayer but doesn't live for Christ as an ongoing lifestyle. They think they are saved, but they are not.

The first time I observed this was that very same summer and fall (1970). There had been a revival of sorts in our high school. If I remember correctly, up to twenty kids had received Christ within a few short weeks because of an undeniable outpouring of God's Spirit. This outpouring touched numerous parents as well, including my own. It was a golden time of prayer meetings, Bible studies, church services and after-meeting fellowship at restaurants among turned-on kids and adults alike. Fast-forward one year, and the number of kids that were genuinely following Christ was down to about a half dozen. What happened?

What happened is not a mystery. Jesus talked about it.

Mark 4:1-10

1   *Again he began to teach beside the sea. And a very large crowd gathered about him, so that he got into a boat and sat in it on the sea, and the whole crowd was beside the sea on the land.*

2   *And he was teaching them many things in parables, and in his teaching he said to them:*

3   *Listen! Behold, a sower went out to sow.*

4   *And as he sowed, some seed fell **along the path**, and the birds came and devoured it.*

5   *Other seed fell on **rocky ground**, where it did not have much soil, and immediately it sprang up, since it had no depth of soil.*

6   *And when the sun rose, it was scorched, and since it had no root, it withered away.*

7   *Other seed fell **among thorns**, and the thorns grew up and choked it, and it yielded no grain.*

8   *And other seeds fell into **good soil** and produced grain, growing up and increasing and yielding thirtyfold and sixtyfold and a hundredfold."*

9   *And he said, "He who has ears to hear, let him hear."*

10   *And when he was alone, those around him with the twelve asked him about the parables.*

His disciples weren't exactly sure what all of this meant, so they asked Jesus, "What gives? What's that all about?" And so Jesus explained the parable to them.

Mark 4:14-20

14 *The sower sows the word.*

15 *And these are the ones along the path, where the word is sown: when they hear, Satan immediately comes and takes away the word that is sown in them.*

16 *And these are the ones sown on rocky ground: the ones who, when they hear the word, immediately receive it with joy.*

17 *And they have no root in themselves, but endure for a while; then, when tribulation or persecution arises on account of the word, immediately they fall away.*

18 *And others are the ones sown among thorns. They are those who hear the word,*

19 *but the cares of the world and the deceitfulness of riches and the desires for other things enter in and choke the word, and it proves unfruitful.*

20 *But those that were sown on the good soil are the ones who hear the word and accept it and bear fruit, thirtyfold and sixtyfold and a hundredfold."*

Jesus lists four different reactions to the Gospel with four different results.

Along the path	Heard - didn't receive - Satan immediately steals the Word of God – they didn't respond at all (Luke 8:12 – not saved).
Rocky ground	Heard - received with joy (Luke 8:13 - believed for a while) - fell away because of persecution or adversity. Saved, but turned away from faith.

Thorns	Heard - (received implied – Luke 8:14 – their fruit does not mature)—but the cares of this world, the deceitfulness of riches, and the desire for other things took precedent and choked out the Word – it became unfruitful. Saved, but turned away from faith.
Good soil	Heard – received – saved- bore fruit.

Out of the three groups that heard and received Christ, only one group **continued** to follow Christ, grow and bear fruit.

The kids from our high school that didn't **continue** with Christ most likely fell away due to a combination of peer pressure (fear of persecution), the cares of this world and the desire for other things. They had good initial intentions, but good intentions didn't result in spiritual growth and faithfulness to Christ..

But that was forty-seven years ago. I've had forty-seven years to keep observing. These observations don't even take into account the myriads of people who intellectually believe in Jesus but have not actually crossed over the line of faith and been genuinely "born again." Churches are full of people who are not and never have been Christ-followers. In other words, they have never invited Jesus Christ into their lives as Lord and Savior in the first place. They are not "saved"—but they THINK they're saved. They think they're saved because their clergy told them growing up that they're saved because they were baptized when they were a few days old, were "confirmed," went to "first holy communion," or participated in some other religious ceremony or ritual. Deceived clergy produce deceived congregants. The problem is endemic.

I thought I was saved until my brother John told me I wasn't. I didn't appreciate being told that. John challenged me on what it meant to be saved and what is required for someone to receive eternal life. There was friction there at first. There is always friction before radical change. Friction can bring heat, light or both. Usually it's heat first, then light. After a couple weeks of heat, the friction produced light, and I accepted Christ. I was told that I had to be "born again," and that meant a personal decision to believe, receive and follow Jesus Christ—that I didn't have eternal life just because I went to church or participated in some religious ceremony.

I grew up Roman Catholic and up until I was seventeen years old thought I was saved just because I was Catholic, had been baptized, experienced first holy communion, was confirmed, was an altar boy, went to confession once in a while and communion every Sunday (my confessions were good for several weeks). I was, therefore, by default, "in." But my brother John told me I wasn't "in"—just being "in" church doesn't make one saved. Corrie Ten Boom (author of *The Hiding Place*) told the story, when she was a young girl, of a man who didn't act Christian. When she quizzed her father about this, he said, "Corrie, just because you find a mouse in the cookie jar doesn't make him a cookie!"

Fast forward eleven or twelve years. Shortly after I started pastoring I had a good friend from high school that died in a car accident because he was drunk. I distinctly remember sitting in that Catholic Church for his funeral, the same one I attended up until I was 20 years old. At his funeral, I heard that my friend, because he had been baptized when he was a few weeks old, found entrance to eternal life. Here are the instructions for the Roman Catholic funeral:

The casket is also blessed with holy water, another reminder of the person's baptism, the day they were first given the promise of eternal life. ... The sprinkling with holy water, which recalls **the person's entrance into eternal life through Baptism. ...** **The person who began life as a Christian disciple in Baptism.**[1]

As I heard those words that my friend was in heaven just because he had been baptized as an infant, my heart sank as I looked around and saw all those people swallowing what the misinformed priest just said. Ugh! My disappointment turned to anger over this lie of the ages—that one is saved and goes to heaven because of a religious ceremony shortly after birth, when

---

[1] https://www.osv.com/Article/TabId/493/ArtMID/13569/ArticleID/10323/What-Every-Catholic-needs-to-know-about-funerals.aspx and http://ordinariate.net/documents/resources/AC_Order_for_Funerals.pdf and ...
http://www.pastoralliturgy.org/resources/BaptismalsymbolsatFunerals.pdf

they have no free will or maturity to decide. It made me angry then and it makes me angry now to know that there are millions of people that have been duped into believing they are saved when they are not.

For forty-seven years now, because of direct conversations, of keeping current on thoughts and trends, of doing a lot of reading, and because of hearing people talk in everyday life, I've been troubled at this lie that the institutional church (Catholic or Protestant) has sold people...*just go through this ceremony, just believe in Jesus and you have eternal life.* If you're Protestant, "just say this sinner's prayer," and everything's going to be just fine. I heard it just recently, *Just repeat this prayer after me and you can know with 100% certainty that you'll have eternal life.* Repentance was not even mentioned.

And that's the genesis of this book. I want to drill down and find out from Scripture what it means to believe in Jesus. What does it mean to believe that Jesus is "Lord" and "Savior?" What does it mean to be born again? What is involved with receiving eternal life? How do we have assurance that we'll stay faithful to Christ?

CHAPTER 2

Nominal Christianity

The problem we have in the United States is *nominal Christianity* and *nominal Christians*. One definition for the word *nominal* is, "existing in name only." Therefore, a nominal Christian is a Christ-follower in name only. They're not really Christ-followers. They think they're saved but they aren't. Our churches are full of them.

I'm a nominal golfer. I don't even call it golf, I call it "connect-the-sand traps." I'm not a real golfer, I'm a nominal golfer, a golfer in name only. A real golfer golfs a lot and takes it seriously, trying to improve their game and give it their all. Not me. I dabble at it once in a while. I like it but I'm not that serious about it. I take a mulligan whenever I jolly well feel like it. I don't even keep score. Real golfers don't do that, so I'm a nominal golfer. That's OK with golf, but it's not OK with Jesus Christ and eternity.

Kyle Idleman, in his book, *I'm Not a Fan,*[2] distinguishes between a *fan* and a *follower*. That's a great way to put it. There are millions of people who are *fans* of Jesus, but they are not *followers*. There is a huge difference between the two. Nominal Christians are fans. True Christians are followers.

One time Jesus said something startling—I mean downright shocking. It runs crosswise to what most people think. In fact, most people don't even know that Jesus said it.

Matthew 7:13-14

*Enter by the narrow gate. For the gate is wide and the way is easy that leads to **destruction**, and those who enter by it are **many**. For the gate is narrow and the way is hard that leads to **life**, and those who find it are **few**.*

---

2   I'm Not A Fan, Kyle Idelman, Zondervan, 2011

```
┌─────────────────────────────────────────┐
│                                         │
│   Many  ──────────▶ Destruction         │
│                                         │
│   Few   ──────────▶ Eternal Life        │
│                                         │
└─────────────────────────────────────────┘
```

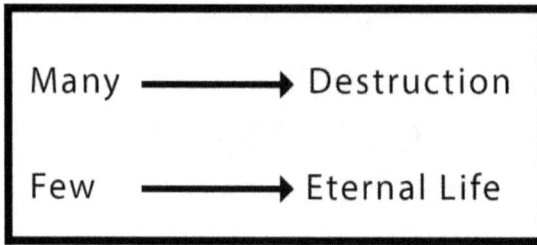

I said this is startling, but why? Because Jesus basically said that the vast majority of people don't go to heaven, only a very few. That's astounding. The impression you get from people is that just about everybody goes to heaven except for obvious serial killers and scumbags. Approximately 85% of all people think they're going to heaven.[3] Either these people are right, or Jesus is right. I'm going with Jesus on this one.

People who think they're going to heaven but aren't, think so for three reasons:

1. They confuse desire with reality.

2. They exaggerate their own goodness.

3. They are products of their teaching. That is, they've been taught that they are going to heaven by priests, pastors who are plainly contradicting the teaching of Christ.

If the verses in Matthew 7 cited above are wild, look down several verses.

Matthew 7:21-22

*Not everyone who says to me, "Lord, Lord," will enter the kingdom of heaven, but the one who does the will of my Father who is in heaven. On that day **many** will say to me, "Lord, Lord, did we not prophesy in your name, and cast out demons in your name, and do many mighty works in your name?" And then will I declare to them, "I **never knew you**; depart from me, you workers of lawlessness."*

---

[3] http://www.huffingtonpost.com/2005/12/20/85-of-americans-think-the_n_12620.html

At judgement, "many" are going to call Jesus "Lord," but He's going to reply, "You call me Lord, but, in reality, your life didn't reflect that I was Lord in your life. Depart from Me."

The people talked about here in Matthew 7 were nominal Christians. They were Christians in name only. They *talked the talk* but didn't *walk the walk*. There are millions of people in this boat, and that's why Jesus called it the *wide* gate.

Some will protest, "But wait, I believe in Jesus!" This is a very common response. But James, in the letter (epistle) of his name, touched on that.

James 2:19

You say you have faith, for you believe that there is one God. Good for you! Even the demons believe this, and they tremble in terror. (NLT)

You believe in Jesus? Good for you, even demons believe. Hell, yes, a real hell, is filled with people who believed in Jesus before they died. I think it should be obvious from this verse that simple intellectual belief is not the same as biblical faith. There is a vast difference between intellectual belief, what we call *mental assent*, and true, biblical faith. The cause of the confusion comes because the word "believe" is used in Scripture, and so, in our 21st century minds, we interpret that word according to normal usage—as mere credence or intellectual belief. We'll see a verse about belief and think to ourselves, "Well shoot, I do that." They'll read John 3:16 and think, "I'm good."

John 3:16

*For God so loved the world, that he gave his only Son, that whoever **believes** in him should not perish but have eternal life.*

People see that and think, "I believe in Christ, therefore I have eternal life." But the people in Matthew 7:21 "believed" in Christ, they even called Him "Lord," but Jesus said to them, "I never knew you."

The problem here is the difference between our English word *believe* and the Greek word for *believe*. The New Testament was written in Greek, so it behooves us to drill down a little deeper to find out what that word "believe" really means versus our contemporary use of it. It is the Greek word, *pisteuō*. Here's its definition:

pisteuō (pis-tú-ō)

> *To place confidence in, an inner conviction that causes one to **trust in, to entrust oneself to** a thing, to **commit to** a truth. Vine's Expository Dictionary of New Testament Words: "**reliance upon, not mere credence.**"*[4]

That is much different, much stronger than just mental assent. John 3:16 in *The Amplified Bible*, which takes Greek words and amplifies and expands them in the translation, reads this way:

John 3:16

> *For God so greatly loved and dearly prized the world that He [even] gave up His only begotten (unique) Son, so that whoever believes in **(trusts in, clings to, relies on)** Him shall not perish (come to destruction, be lost) but have eternal (everlasting) life. (Amplified Bible Classic Edition)*

Trusts in, clings to, relies on...is much different then mental assent or mere credence. It's the same exact Greek word translated "entrust" in Luke 16:11.

Luke 16:11

> *If then you have not been faithful in the unrighteous wealth, who will **entrust** to you the true riches?*

The word is translated "entrust" in many translations because it's a word that means "to commit to another with confidence."[5] The same word "believe" in John 3:16 is "entrust" in Luke 16:11.

The Greek definition of "believes" here in Scripture is: "trusts in, clings to, relies on." It's not the same as mere credence—merely intellectually believing in something. It's the kind of belief that results in a person throwing themselves wholly into something.

---

[4]   https://www.blueletterbible.org/lang/lexicon/lexi-con.cfm?Strongs=G4100&t=KJV

[5]   https://www.merriam-webster.com/dictionary/entrust

Nominal Christians are those with mere credence in Jesus. They are the Matthew 7:21 people. True Christians are those who believe in Jesus Christ so as to trust in Him, cling to Him, rely upon Him, and place their confidence in Him on a regular and *continuing* basis, in other words...as a lifestyle, not a one-time decision. This belief causes them to actively surrender to and *follow* Jesus Christ, not merely intellectually believe in Him (more on this later).

The Lausanne Committee for World Evangelization (LCWE) is a think-tank group based in Lausanne, Switzerland. They met to tackle head-on the problem of nominal Christians.

The Lausanne Committee for World Evangelization (LCWE) defines a nominal Christian as "a person who has not responded in repentance and faith to Jesus Christ as his personal Savior and Lord." The LCWE notes that such a one "may be a practicing or non-practicing church member. He may give intellectual assent to basic Christian doctrines and claim to be a Christian. He may be faithful in attending liturgical rites and worship services, and be an active member involved in church affairs." The LCWE also suggests that nominal Christianity "is to be found wherever the church is more than one generation old."[6]

Nominal Christians are everywhere. They attend church, engage in liturgical rites, are church members, even church leaders. But they are Christians in name only, and they are not saved. Jesus said so.

---

6   https://en.wikipedia.org/wiki/Nominal_Christian

CHAPTER 3

What It Means to be 'Born Again' – Repent and Believe

The term "born again" these days is used to describe everything from a company reinventing itself, to a washed-up actor hitting it big again. Society has taken a phrase first used by Jesus Christ with a very specific meaning, and watered it down to mean virtually nothing much at all, "I've used this shampoo and conditioner for the last week and I feel born again!" We owe it to ourselves to see how Jesus used this term and what He meant by it.

John 3:1-7

1   Now there was a man of the Pharisees named Nicodemus, a ruler of the Jews.

2   This man came to Jesus by night and said to him, "Rabbi, we know that you are a teacher come from God, for no one can do these signs that you do unless God is with him."

3   Jesus answered him, "Truly, truly, I say to you, unless one is **born again** he cannot see the kingdom of God."

4   Nicodemus said to him, "How can a man be born when he is old? Can he enter a second time into his mother's womb and be born?"

5   Jesus answered, "Truly, truly, I say to you, unless one is **born of water and the Spirit**, he cannot enter the kingdom of God.

⁶   *That which is born of the flesh is flesh, and that which is born of the Spirit is spirit.*

⁷   *Do not marvel that I said to you, 'You must be **born again.**'"*

Here the term used by Jesus is not mere intellectual belief, but an experience—being born of the Spirit, a spiritual rebirth into a new life.

Jesus said to see (enter into) the kingdom of God a person must be born of water and of the Spirit. "Born of water" is a reference to our first or natural birth. In that birth, the baby is surrounded by water in the amniotic sac. When it's time for the birth, the amniotic sac ruptures and water (amniotic fluid) comes out. The mother will recount the event by saying something like "my water broke at three in the afternoon on Monday."

My son, Jesse, was born six weeks early, on a Saturday. That day I had to attend Bible school classes in the morning about a forty-minute drive away from Rochester, New York (Elim Bible Institute and College). That morning I got up early to get dressed and ready to head out. As I was getting ready my wife Debby came into the bedroom from the bathroom and said that she believed her "water had just broken." I told her that can't be because she wasn't due for six more weeks. I told her that she probably just had an accident in the bathroom and to relax, not worry about it, and go back to bed. She did, and I left. While in class I got a note that read, "Your wife is in the hospital having a baby." OK, OK, so I was wrong, you're "water did break."

This is natural birth, birth number one, "born of water." Jesus describes this birth by saying, "That which is born of the flesh is flesh." "Born of the flesh" therefore is what Jesus was talking about when He said "born of water."

But Jesus mentioned a second birth, being "born of the Spirit." It is no less an event than our first birth. It is not a belief, it is an event. My wife didn't have a baby because she "believed" she had a baby, she had a baby because of a real space-time experience. Jesus said, "That which is born of the Spirit (capital "S" meaning the Holy Spirit) is spirit (small "s," meaning the newly recreated spirit of man)."

1 Peter 1:23

*For you have been **born again**, not of perishable seed, but of imperishable, through the living and enduring word of God.*

The seed that produced your first birth was from your biological father, but the second birth, the spiritual birth, is from the imperishable seed of God Himself, meaning, it's a supernatural event.

Our first birth resulted in new life. Our second birth results in new life as well.

2 Corinthians 5:17

Therefore, if anyone is in Christ, he is a new creation. The old has passed away; behold, the new has come.

There is a "God-side" and a "man-side" to this event of being born again. It's not all God (though Calvinists would disagree) and it's not all man. Let me explain.

God is the One who woos, touches, influences and draws a person by the Holy Spirit to recognize their need for Christ and salvation, and takes them to the point of decision with full conviction.

John 6:44

No one can come to me unless the Father who sent me draws him.

The born-again experience is a supernatural event or experience that is initiated by a supernatural God. God's grace moves upon an individual and touches their heart, resulting in the individual's recognition of their sin and their need of a Savior. In theology, it's called "prevenient grace." *Prevenient* means "preceding or happening before." God does something BEFORE we do something. He initiates.

Acts 16:14

*One who heard us was a woman named Lydia, from the city of Thyatira, a seller of purple goods, who was a worshiper of God. **The Lord opened her heart** to pay attention to what was said by Paul.*

15

Luke 24:31

And **their eyes were opened**, and they recognized him.

Luke 24:45

Then **he opened their minds** to understand the Scriptures.

This is the "God-side" of the born-again experience, this is prevenient grace, God touching and influencing someone's heart to hear, understand and respond to the gospel.

The "man-side" of being born again is that, even though God is touching and influencing a person's heart, a person must still choose to respond to God's gracious invitation by making a decision. This involves doing a cost-benefit analysis and then making a choice.

Luke 14:25-33

25   *Now great crowds accompanied him, and he turned and said to them,*

26   *"If anyone comes to me and does not hate his own father and mother and wife and children and brothers and sisters, yes, and even his own life, he cannot be my disciple.*

27   *Whoever does not bear his own cross and come after me cannot be my disciple.*

28   *For which of you, desiring to build a tower, does not first sit down and count the cost, whether he has enough to complete it?*

29   *Otherwise, when he has laid a foundation and is not able to finish, all who see it begin to mock him,*

30   *saying, 'This man began to build and was not able to finish.'*

31   *Or what king, going out to encounter another king in war, will not sit down first and deliberate whether he is able with ten thousand to meet him who comes against him with twenty thousand?*

32   And if not, while the other is yet a great way off, he sends a delegation and asks for terms of peace.

33   So therefore, any one of you who does not renounce all that he has cannot be my disciple.

This perfectly describes the cost-benefit analysis involved in making a decision to follow Christ. Here, Jesus is clearly teaching that we should count the cost before deciding. There is nowhere in this passage that says or implies that the person is forced to make a decision independent of free-will. If a decision was forced upon someone there would be no need to instruct us to count the cost. So even though God touches and opens the heart of an individual, thereby wooing and drawing them to the Savior, they must still count the cost and make a decision. This is the "man-side" of the born-again experience. The Spirit acts on man's heart and issues an invitation, and man must choose to accept or reject that invitation. But what is involved with this decision? What are we, in fact, deciding to do?

WHAT THE 'BORN AGAIN' DECISION INVOLVES

The decision to be born again involves four things:

1. Repent
2. Believe
3. Receive
4. Follow

This takes a somewhat fuzzy or ambiguous decision criteria of what it means to be born again, to something that is quite specific and clear. I say, "quite clear" even though, in reality, rarely does a pastor or anyone else talk about these elements as they lead people to Christ, which, in my opinion, is untenable. Let me describe each component wrapped up in the decision to be born again.

1. REPENT

The very first command to people from the lips of John the Baptist, Jesus and the Apostle Peter when exhorting people was "repent."

Mark 1:15 – John the Baptist

*The time is fulfilled, and the kingdom of God is at hand; **repent** and believe in the gospel.*

Matthew 3:2 - Jesus

***Repent**, for the kingdom of heaven is at hand.*

Acts 2:38

*And Peter said to them, "**Repent** and be baptized every one of you in the name of Jesus Christ for the forgiveness of your sins, and you will receive the gift of the Holy Spirit.*

Even the Apostle Paul, after explaining what God was like to a big crowd, described what God wanted people to do in response to the gospel message.

Acts 17:30

*The times of ignorance God overlooked, but now he commands all people everywhere to **repent**.*

Acts 20:21

*Testifying both to Jews and to Greeks of **repentance** toward God and of faith in our Lord Jesus Christ.*

The author of Hebrews, in chapter 6, lists six major doctrines that believers should have "under their belts" so that they can move on to deeper doctrines of the Christian faith.

Hebrews 6:1-2

*Therefore let us leave the elementary doctrine of Christ and go on to maturity, not laying again a foundation of **repentance from dead works** and of faith toward God, and of instruction about washings, the laying on of hands, the resurrection of the dead, and eternal judgment.*

The very first foundational doctrine mentioned here is *repentance from dead works.*

Then in the book of Revelation, in chapters 2 and 3, when Jesus addressed each church, we see Him issuing a command in each case.

Revelation 2:5

*Remember therefore from where you have fallen; **repent**, and do the works you did at first. If not, I will come to you and remove your lampstand from its place, unless you **repent**.*

Revelation 2:16

*Therefore **repent**. If not, I will come to you soon and war against them with the sword of my mouth.*

Revelation 2:21-22

*I gave her time to **repent**, but she refuses to **repent** of her sexual immorality. Behold, I will throw her onto a sickbed, and those who commit adultery with her I will throw into great tribulation, unless they **repent** of her works.*

Revelation 3:3

*Remember, then, what you received and heard. Keep it, and **repent**. If you will not wake up, I will come like a thief, and you will not know at what hour I will come against you.*

Revelation 3:19

*Those whom I love, I reprove and discipline, so be zealous and **repent**.*

Whereas the previous verses were directing repentance toward the sinner, here in Revelation Jesus is directing repentance toward Christians. If you're not careful, you'll almost get the impression that repentance is a big deal, both to sinner and believer alike (said facetiously).

Most people don't have a clue about what the word *repent* or *repentance* really means. The word "repent" in the Greek language, *metanoeō*, literally means "to change one's mind and direction." We tend to think repent means to have remorse for one's sin, but this is wrong.

Matthew 27:3 says that Judas, after betraying Jesus and turning Him in to the Jewish and Roman authorities, "was seized with remorse." The Greek word used here for *remorse* is *metamelomai* which means "to regret." Matthew didn't use the normal biblical word for "repentance," *metanoeō*, "a change of mind resulting in a change of direction." Remorse is not repentance, it is simply feeling regret for something one did.

When we view repentance in light of all the entirety of Scripture, we come to understand that repentance contains six major elements.

Thomas Watson (1620-1686) was a Puritan preacher who lived in England. He was well educated and author of quite a few books. One book Watson authored is, *The Doctrine of Repentance*. He lists six components of true repentance which I'll put in my own words and with a slight change of Watson's order.

WHAT REPENTANCE ENTAILS:

1. **Recognition of sin.**
   - In the story of the Prodigal son, it says in Luke 15:17, "But when he came to himself..."
   - 2 Timothy 2:25-26 talks about us correcting people that, "God may perhaps grant them repentance leading to a knowledge of the truth, and they may come to their senses."
   - One can't repent of sin not recognized as such.
   - The first step of repentance is to come to one's senses and have recognition of sin.

2. **Shame for sin.**

- "Shame" can mean a feeling of embarrassment, disgrace and humiliation for something.
- In Luke 21:15, the Prodigal son said to his father, "Father, I have sinned against heaven and before you. I am no longer worthy to be called your son." This denotes that he felt shame or humiliation.
- Ezekiel 43:10 – "As for you, son of man, describe to the house of Israel the temple, that **they may be ashamed of their iniquities**; and they shall measure the plan."
- Repenting people sense shame but those who are stiff-necked and unrepentant feel no shame. Zephaniah 3:5 – "**the unjust knows no shame.**"
- Jeremiah 6:15 – "Were they ashamed when they committed abomination? No, they were not at all ashamed; **they did not know how to blush.**"
- Ezra 9:5-6: "And at the evening sacrifice I rose from my fasting, with my garment and my cloak torn, and fell upon my knees and spread out my hands to the Lord my God, saying: 'O my God, **I am ashamed and blush** to lift my face to you, my God, for our iniquities have risen higher than our heads, and our guilt has mounted up to the heavens.'"
- I wonder how many who said "the sinner's prayer" didn't blush and didn't express shame for their past sin? How many skipped right over this?

3. **Godly sorrow.**
   - One can feel shame, humiliation and embarrassment over one's sin (as they should), but still not in actuality sense sorrow for that act.
   - When I was in eighth grade, I was kicked out of school for stealing money out of wallets in the locker room from the lockers of the visiting basketball team. The vice-principal came into the cafeteria and in front of all the other students, called out me and three friends to go to the office. I felt shame. I don't remember feeling actual sorrow.
   - Sorrow is not regret for getting caught, it is godly sorrow for having transgressed God's commandments and offending a holy God. Sorrow produces real brokenness.

21

- Psalm 51:17 – "The sacrifices of God are a broken spirit; a broken and contrite heart, O God, you will not despise."
- 2 Corinthians 7:9, 10 – "I now rejoice, not that you were made sorrowful, but that you were made sorrowful to the point of repentance; for you were made sorrowful according to the will of God...For the sorrow that is according to the will of God produces a repentance without regret, leading to salvation." NASB

4. **Confession**
   - Psalm 38:18 – "I confess my iniquity; I am sorry for my sin."
   - 1 John 1:9 – "If we confess our sins, he is faithful and just to forgive us our sins and to cleanse us from all unrighteousness." (Reference Psalm 32:3-5)
   - Psalm 32:3, 5 – "For when I kept silent, my bones wasted away... I acknowledged my sin to you, and I did not cover my iniquity; I said, 'I will confess my transgressions to the Lord," and you forgave the iniquity of my sin.'"

5. **Hatred of sin.**
   - One must hate sin before he forsakes it.
   - Psalm 97:10 – "O you who love the Lord, hate evil!"
   - Proverbs 8:13 – "The fear of the Lord is hatred of evil."
   - We must come to see sin through God's eyes. You'll never be delivered from a sin you love. You must come to hate it.
   - Romans 12:9 – "Abhor what is evil."

6. **Change of mind/direction**
   - Matthew 3:8 – "Bear fruit in keeping with repentance."
   - The words above were spoken by John the Baptist who was speaking to the Pharisees and Sadducees when they supposedly "repented" and were in line to be baptized. John the Baptist knew they were repenting simply as a religious show, but had no intention of real life-change.

- Isaiah 55:7 – "Let the wicked forsake his way, and the unrighteous man his thoughts; **let him return to the Lord**, that he may have compassion on him, and to our God, for he will abundantly pardon."
- Acts 26:20 – "That they should repent and **turn to God, performing deeds in keeping with their repentance.**"
- Repentance is turning away from something while at the same time turning to God. Turning away but not turning toward God is not repentance.

Repentance is the missing ingredient in almost all altar calls or personal evangelistic appeals for people to accept Christ. Jesus' command in Mark 1:15 is "repent and believe."

Yet, public altar calls almost universally skip repentance and shoot straight for believing and faith. In fact, I don't remember an altar call that stressed repentance for one's sins, and that includes all the altar calls I gave! This is why so few converts become disciples. They have skipped over the very first command from Scripture, repent, and suckered into an "easy believe-ism."

Preaching repentance is not popular. It cost John the Baptist his life. English preacher Joseph Parker (1830-1902), in his book, *These Sayings of Mine – Pulpit Notes on Seven Chapters of the First Gospel, and Other Sermons*, talks about this unpopular subject...repentance. In talking about John the Baptist, he writes:

"The man whose little sermon is 'repent' sets himself against his age, and will for the time being be battered mercilessly by the age whose moral tone he challenges. There is but one end for such a man — 'off with his head!' You had better not try to preach repentance until you have pledged your head to heaven."[7]

This is why it's not covered much these days.

So the decision to be born again involves four things, number 1—repent. But let's move on.

---

[7] Joseph Parker - http://ow.ly/JNZm30dAoY7

2. BELIEVE

The second component of becoming born again is to believe.

Mark 1:15

*The time is fulfilled, and the kingdom of God is at hand; **repent** and **believe** in the gospel.*

Hebrews 6:1-2

*Therefore let us leave the elementary doctrine of Christ and go on to maturity, not laying again a foundation of **repentance** from dead works and of **faith** toward God.*

As stated earlier in Chapter 2, believe (faith) does not mean mental or intellectual assent. It is the type of belief that results in one throwing themselves wholly into the truth so that it becomes a commitment to a thing. It is reliance and trust in, not mere credence. I won't spend time on this now because the entirety of this book teases out the implication of this word *believe*.

Repent and believe are the first two critical components of being born again. In the next chapter, we'll look at two more.

Chapter 4

What It Means to be 'Born Again' – Receive and Follow

Jesus said in John 3:3, ""Truly, truly, I say to you, unless one is **born again** he cannot see the kingdom of God." But what does born again mean? What does the decision entail? In the last chapter we looked at the first two components of this decision—repent and believe. But there are two more components of being born again that we need to delve into.

3. RECEIVE

A critical component of being born again is "receiving" Jesus Christ into one's life as Lord and Savior.

John 1:12

*But to all who did **receive** him, who **believed** in his name, he gave the right to become children of God.*

Two things are mentioned here, *believe* and *receive*. It's not just believing in Christ, it is receiving Christ.

"Receiving" means taking Jesus Christ into one's life as both Lord and Savior. We'll define these titles in detail later in this book. Suffice it to say for now, that receiving Christ into one's life as "Lord" means making a decision to step down from the throne of one's life and inviting Jesus Christ to sit on that throne, being the head over one's life. In other words, there is a surrendering to the Lordship, rulership and leadership of Jesus Christ over one's life. It's a step beyond just believing.

Acts 11:21

*And the hand of the Lord was with them, and a great number who believed **turned to the Lord**.*

"Believe" means "turning to the Lord." Believing of course is great, but here we take the next step and turn to the Lord, which means receiving Him into one's life as Lord and Savior. It involves a personal surrendering to Him as Ruler over one's life.

Receiving Jesus Christ as "Savior" denotes that one is trusting in Christ's redeeming work on the cross to take upon Himself their sin, and grant to them salvation by grace alone, through faith alone.

In John 1:12, the word "receive" (all who did *receive* Him) is the Greek word *lambanō*, and means "to take or lay hold of." For example, in Acts 27:35, when Paul urged the men on the ship to stop fasting and to eat something, it says, "And when he had said these things, he **took** (*lambanō*) bread, and giving thanks to God in the presence of all he broke it and began to eat." The word "took" here is the same Greek word as "received" in John 1:12. What did Paul do? He took the break into his hands, in other words, he *laid hold of it*, he grabbed onto it. We must personally take and lay hold of Christ at the point of being born again.

When someone gives you a gift, it's not in your personal possession until you take, lay hold of it and bring it to yourself, even if prior to taking it, you believed it was yours. This is what happens in the born-again experience. Christ is offered to us by the Father, but we must lay hold of Christ and personally receive Him into our lives as Lord and Savior.

4. FOLLOW

Lastly, part of the experience of being born again is a sincere decision to *follow* Jesus Christ. "Follow" is an action verb. "Follow" is actually part and parcel of number 3 above, "receive." The act of receiving is simultaneously both the decision to invite Christ into one's life as Lord and Savior and then to actively follow Him. Inviting Christ in with no intention or decision of following Him is empty, void and powerless.

Matthew 8:18-22

18   *Now when Jesus saw a crowd around him, he gave orders to go over to the other side.*

19   *And a scribe came up and said to him, "Teacher, I will **follow** you wherever you go."*

20   *And Jesus said to him, "Foxes have holes, and birds of the air have nests, but the Son of Man has nowhere to lay his head."*

21   *Another of the disciples said to him, "Lord, let me first go and bury my father."*

22   *And Jesus said to him, "**Follow me**, and leave the dead to bury their own dead."*

Jesus' invitation to us is to follow Him, not just believe in Him. The decision to be born again is a decision to follow, not just believe. Verse 22 always grabs me. Can you imagine saying to someone whose father just died—"Let the spiritually dead bury the physically dead, your priority is to follow Me"? Jesus here is clearly teaching what truly believing in Him entails...following.

If you think what Jesus said to that person whose father just passed away was brutal, it gets wilder.

Matthew 10:34-39

34   *"Do not think that I have come to bring peace to the earth. I have not come to bring peace, but a sword.*

35   *For I have come to set a man against his father, and a daughter against her mother, and a daughter-in-law against her mother-in-law.*

36   *And a person's enemies will be those of his own household.*

37   *Whoever loves father or mother more than me is not worthy of me, and whoever loves son or daughter more than me is not worthy of me.*

38   *And whoever does not take his cross and **follow me** is not worthy of me.*

*39   Whoever finds his life will lose it, and whoever loses his life
for my sake will find it.*

I wonder if the above passage is ever read and explained during an altar call, before people raise their hands or come forward. I don't have to wonder...it's not. We jump right to the "If you believe in Jesus and want eternal life, signify this by raising your hand." No mention of what this decision entails.

But Jesus clearly and unambiguously communicates to us what the decision to be born again means, and it includes a cost-benefit analysis. "Follow me" is no lightweight decision.

In the story of the rich young ruler in Mark 10, the man asked Jesus what he needed to do to experience eternal life. The man *thought* he was willing to do whatever it took to experience it and was quite proud of it. But he found out differently. After touting his own goodness, a greatly exaggerated goodness, Jesus throws down the real test to the man.

Mark 10:21-22

*And Jesus, looking at him, loved him, and said to him, "You lack one thing: go, sell all that you have and give to the poor, and you will have treasure in heaven; and come, **follow me**." Disheartened by the saying, he went away sorrowful, for he had great possessions.*

The man found out that experiencing eternal life included the decision to follow Christ **at all costs, above all things**. He declined the offer. In a way, I admire the man because at least he did the cost-benefit analysis and was honest enough to decide against it. In altar calls, we don't even mention the cost. This produces more numbers, more people "saved." But greater numbers of converts (I use the term loosely) don't translate to greater numbers of true disciples.

Part of "following" Jesus Christ includes "obeying." The decision to follow Jesus is simultaneously a decision to do what He says. We just can't separate loving and following from obeying.

John 15:10

If you keep my commandments, you will abide in my love, just as I have kept my Father's commandments and abide in his love.

John 14:15

If you love me, you will keep my commandments.

John 14:23

Jesus answered him, "If anyone loves me, he will keep my word, and my Father will love him, and we will come to him and make our home with him.

1 John 5:3

For this is the love of God, that we keep his commandments.

There is no such thing as loving or following Jesus without doing what He says. To declare love for Him while being disobedient is a total contradiction.

1 John 1:6

If we say we have fellowship with him while we walk in darkness, we lie and do not practice the truth.

Following Christ doesn't just mean believing in Him and studying about Him. The essence of following Christ and becoming a disciple is becoming like Him, and you can't do that while disobeying Him.

Last week (at the time of this writing) I sat in the room at an assisted living facility and chatted with a dear lady who maybe had two weeks to live because of cancer (and she knew it). In the past, I'd prayed with this dear woman to receive Christ and be born again. On this occasion, she admitted to me the sin of adultery at a much earlier age. I asked if she'd ever repented for this sin, and she said no, at which point I led her in a prayer of repentance. She cried and felt wonderful. So far, so good.

Later in the conversion I discovered that she had some real bitterness and unforgiveness toward a certain lady in a different state. I took quite a bit of time talking about the need to let go and forgive. I took her to the Lord's prayer, "forgive us our trespasses AS WE forgive those who have trespassed against us." I read to her from Mark 11.

Mark 11:25

> *And whenever you stand praying, forgive, if you have anything against anyone, so that your Father also who is in heaven may forgive you your trespasses."*

I explained that if she didn't forgive this lady that God couldn't forgive her. I explained that forgiveness is not based on the person's actions, but totally on the love of God inside of us, who forgave us when we were guilty in our sins (Romans 5:8 – "God shows his love for us in that while we were still sinners, Christ died for us."). I explained that letting go and forgiving someone is not a feeling, it's a choice.

When I asked her if she was willing to forgive this lady, to my surprise she said "no." I said, "If Jesus was personally standing right in front of you right now, and told you that He wanted you to forgive this lady, would you?" She said, "I don't think I could." I was shocked. I was glad she was honest, but wow, claiming to be born again but openly admitting she wouldn't forgive this lady even if Jesus appeared to her and commanded her to do so? Wow. The end of the story is, a week later she called our office crying (and got my wife Debby, the receptionist, crying), saying she had forgiven this lady, and everyone else for that matter. Within a week after that she passed away.

Following means obeying. And sure, there will be lots of times we sin by disobeying, but still, when we look at our lives as a whole, is it marked by obedience? If not, we need to question if we're truly born again, or maybe just said a quick "sinner's prayer" with no *continuing* coupled with *obedience*. In describing those in heaven who had their father's name written on their foreheads, it says:

Revelation 14:1, 4

> *Then I looked, and behold, on Mount Zion stood the Lamb, and with him 144,000 who had his name and his Father's name written on their foreheads. ... It is these who **follow the Lamb wherever he goes.***

Becoming born again involves the decision to follow the Lamb wherever He goes, and doing whatever He says.

In concluding these two chapters about what it means to be born again, I need to clarify something important. Very few of us, at the time we were born again, fully knew what was involved with that decision. But spiritual growth requires that we progressively understand, embrace and walk in the light of these components. I repented when I accepted Christ, but I repent now whenever I sin. I believed when I accepted Christ, but I continue to press into that belief and trust in Him even more strongly now. I received and laid hold of Christ at the time I was born again, but now I lay hold of Him daily. I began to follow Christ when I was born again, but I make the decision to follow Him daily.

So even if we didn't fully comprehend all the components of what it means to be born again, we must decide to embrace and walk in these four things as a lifestyle daily: repent, believe, receive and follow. The moment of being born again is just the start of walking in the reality of those things. It is the beginning of the salvation journey, not the end. More on 'salvation as a journey' later.

"The chief danger that confronts the coming century will be religion without the Holy Ghost, Christianity without Christ, **forgiveness without repentance, salvation without regeneration,** *politics without God, heaven without hell."*

- William Booth, Founder of The Salvation Army

Chapter 5

The Problem of False Conversions

There is something called 'false conversions,' and it's a big problem, I would classify it as endemic. A false conversion is when someone thinks they're saved but they are not. They went to church, they responded to an altar call, they said a prayer or repeated some words, but in all reality, they didn't truly engage in the things which typify a true conversion:

1. Repent
2. Believe
3. Receive
4. Follow

They went through some religious motions but they were just that, motions without reality. It's easy, especially with religious practice, to go through the motions. Jesus and the Apostle Paul talked about this.

Matthew 15:8

This people honors me with their lips, but their heart is far from me.

2 Timothy 3:5

Having the appearance of godliness, but denying its power.

To say that the problem of false conversions is pervasive is an understatement. Society and our churches are filled with people who engage in some modicum of religiosity but have no intention of truly following Jesus Christ—acknowledging His Lordship over their lives. They have been inoculated with watered-down religion and subsequently avoid true "religion that God our Father accepts as pure and faultless (James 1:27 NIV)."

These people were led to believe by some well-meaning pastor or Christian, that if they raised their hand, came forward and just said the magic words (the sinner's prayer), they'd miss hell and gain eternal life. Their goal was fire insurance, not a life surrendered and committed to the rulership of Jesus Christ. The reason that the prayer didn't "take" was because it was built on a man-centered gospel instead of the foundation of Jesus Christ.

Ephesians 2:20

*Built on **the foundation** of the apostles and prophets, **Christ Jesus himself being the cornerstone.***

Because they did not truly repent, believe and lay hold of Christ, they did not end up following Him as Lord and Ruler of their life. Chances are, this happened because the decision was not fully explained to them or what it entailed, and therefore they didn't do the cost-benefit analysis talked about in Luke 14:25-33 (count the cost **before** becoming a disciple).

So, is this true? Could it really be that there are many people who think they're saved but really aren't? Most assuredly yes.

Matthew 7:21-23

21 *Not everyone who says to me, "Lord, Lord," will enter the kingdom of heaven, but the one who **does the will of my Father** who is in heaven.*

22 *On that day **many** will say to me, "Lord, Lord, did we not prophesy in your name, and cast out demons in your name, and do many mighty works in your name?"*

23 *And then will I declare to them, "**I never knew you**; depart from me, you **workers of lawlessness**."*

Here we have people who thought they were saved, but weren't. And here Jesus uses the word *many*—"on that day **many** will say to me," which denotes that this problem of false conversions doesn't affect just a few people, but many.

"On that day" signifies the day of judgment, at which time there will be a myriad of people who will be utterly shocked that they weren't granted eternal life and subsequently are forced to do an about-face to begin their journey to, well, a different destination.

These people participated in religious activities and even called Jesus "Lord," but they were not saved.

Saying that Jesus is Lord does not mean one's life reflects that He, in reality, holds the place of *Lord*.

It's not that these people were saved and then lost their salvation, for Jesus said, "I **never** knew you." He didn't say "I knew you at one time but now I don't know you anymore." These people were never saved in the first place. But again, they thought they were!

Question: What was the litmus test identified in this biblical passage that gave evidence they weren't saved? Answer: If you looked at their lives as a whole, they didn't manifest real life-change or true submission to the Lordship of Christ. Their lives didn't express a serious commitment to Christ and subsequent obedience to His commands. In fact, they "did their own thing," didn't do the will of the Father, and engaged in "lawlessness." What is "lawlessness?"

The word "lawlessness" in verse 23 is the Greek word *anomia*. It's a compound word, comprised of *a* (without) and *nomos* (law). These people were "without law," in other words, God's laws didn't govern their lives. They ruled their lives untethered from God's laws or Lordship. Their lives didn't reflect an ongoing submission to God's rulership over their lives. Their lives didn't exemplify submission to God's commandments (remember John 14:15, *If you love me, you will keep my commandments*).

Matthew 7:21-23 clearly shows there are many people who think they're saved, but they are not. The Apostle Paul, in his letter to Titus, confirms this.

Titus 1:16

*They profess to know God, but **they deny him by their works**.*

Here is the principle:

Profession ≠ Possession

And looking at the words of Jesus, they deny their profession of faith how? The answer—by their works, which were a contradiction to their profession. Jesus addressed this reality when speaking to church-going people in Sardis who had the same problem.

Revelation 3:1

I know your works. ***You have the reputation of being alive, but you are dead.***

To me, that is an amazing verse. Jesus said to the church at Sardis: "Everybody thinks you're saved, but you're not, you're dead!" And keep in mind, this was said to church-going people! What was it about some of these people in the church at Sardis that made Jesus say this? Verse 4 clues us in.

Revelation 3:4

Yet you have still a few names in Sardis, people who ***have not soiled (KJV – defiled) their garments.***

"Soiled their garments" doesn't mean digestive problems, it means they were filthy because of defilement and contamination with the world.

James 1:27

Religion that God our Father accepts as pure and faultless is this: to look after orphans and widows in their distress and to keep oneself from ***being polluted by the world.***

Naming Christ but living a life contaminated by the world is how Jesus defined people who "are dead."

In all three of these scriptural references (Matthew 7:21-23, Titus 1:16, Revelation 3:1), the thing that identified these people as not being saved was their works or deeds. In other words, it wasn't their *talk*, it was their *walk* that disqualified them. If one professes Christ, but they are not living in holiness or walking with Jesus as the Lord (obeying His commandments), they are either one of two things...deceived or lying. We're not talking here about being perfect or occasionally sinning, we're talking about a lifestyle of disregard for Christ and His rulership over their lives.

2 Timothy 3:13

*Evil people and impostors will go on from bad to worse, deceiving and **being deceived.***

1 John 1:6

*If we <u>say</u> we have fellowship with him while we <u>walk</u> in darkness, **we lie** and do not practice the truth.*

It's just as simple and clear as that. The two key words here in 1 John 1:6 are "say" compared to "walk." If your *walk* contradicts your *talk*, you're either deceived or lying, one or the other.

It's important to point out, however, that we're not saved by our good works.

Titus 3:5

*He saved us, **not because of works done by us in righteousness**, but according to his own mercy, by the washing of regeneration and renewal of the Holy Spirit*

Galatians 2:16

*Yet we know that a person is **not justified by works of the law** but through faith in Jesus Christ, so we also have believed in Christ Jesus, in order to be justified by faith in Christ and not by works of the law, because by works of the law no one will be justified.*

Ephesians 2:8,9

*For by grace you have been saved through faith. And this is not your own doing; it is the gift of God, **not a result of works**, so that no one may boast.*

We're not saved by works, yet works are *the evidence* of a true, genuine and biblical faith.

James 2:18

*Now someone may argue, "Some people have faith; others have good deeds." But I say, "How can you show me your faith if you don't have good deeds? I will show you my faith **by my good deeds.**"*

We're saved by grace alone through faith alone. However, a true faith will result in works. Here is the overriding principle.

> Faith is the root, works are the fruit.

We don't work FOR our salvation, we work FROM our salvation. We're not saved BY good works, we're saved FOR good works.

Ephesians 2:10

*For we are his workmanship, created in Christ Jesus **for good works**, which God prepared beforehand, that we should walk in them.*

Again, we're not saved by good works, but God has created us so that once saved, He has good works for us to do. These good works are empowered by the Holy Spirit.

If the works aren't present (as we look at a person's life as a whole, over the long haul), we have good reason to believe that the person doesn't possess true, biblical faith, and therefore is not saved.

The problem of false conversions is real and widespread in our churches. And if you think it's wrong to make such a deduction about someone's life, go back and look earlier in Matthew 7. Verses 16-20 confirm Jesus is talking about people whose conduct belies their profession of faith. We'll cover this in Chapter 8 referencing the Book of James. But first, if it's possible for someone to think they're saved but never were...is it possible for someone who genuinely DID get born again, but later reject Christ and His offer of salvation and eternal life?

Chapter 6

The Problem of Genuine Conversions Forfeited

The topic of the last chapter dealt with false conversions, that is, people who may have gone through some motions of believing in Christ, but were never truly born again. They *professed* Christ but didn't *possess* Christ. Jesus said to them, "I NEVER knew you." In other words, they had an intellectual belief in the facts of Jesus Christ, what we call mental assent, but they never had actually *repented*, *believed*, *received* and *followed* Him as a continued lifestyle.

All of this begs another question, "Is it possible for someone to experience a genuine conversion, and then at some later point, by choice, reject, defect or fall away from Christ?" A question that naturally arises along with this question is, "If that's possible, what are the ramifications? Do they forfeit their salvation and eternal life?" These are no small questions. Its relevance affects many people whose eternities are at stake.

We must add to those dicey questions another one, "If all of this is true, does it also apply to those who don't necessarily backslide into the regular practice or lifestyle of sin or an intentional rejection of Christ, but simply live a spiritually passionless life which is void of faithful following and obedience to Christ?" This question touches on those who, after accepting Christ, shrink back from intentionally and purposely pressing on into real discipleship and spiritual growth into a state of lukewarmness. They live as though they still intellectually believe in Christ, but there is no evidence of a living, vibrant faith that bears fruit. There's no evidence of discipleship. And so, what about them?

These deep questions have been debated for two thousand years. They've been addressed by men and women on both sides of the issues, all of whom having initials after their names, i.e., people with deep academic pedigrees. I'm not foolish enough to believe I'm going to solve the debate. Yet, in a book like this, touching on the issues it does, I would be remiss for not addressing these questions and showing from Scripture where I land on them. There are well-known biblical scholars on both sides of these issues whom I have immense respect for. And yet, when I do a plain reading of scripture, there are consistent answers to these things, and the arguments against them seem very weak to me, even if made by well-known scholars. So, with a great deal of respect for those of opposing views, and with fear and trembling, I wade into it.

I'm a firm believer that God had Scripture written for the common man, interpreted with plain reading and meaning. And though there are times when a deeper study of word definitions and cultural background are warranted, for the most part, we should interpret Scripture using plain reading and meaning. With the exceptions of obvious metaphor, allegory and parable, scripture should be taken as it reads without having to perform some interpretive or hermeneutical gymnastics.

Calvinists (reformed theology) answer the question, "Can someone who genuinely accepted Christ and was born again reject Christ and forfeit their salvation?" with a firm, "No!" They advocate for the position "once saved, always saved," or for short, OSAS. It's also known as **unconditional eternal security**. It's *unconditional* because they say once genuinely accepting Christ, eternal life does not have any further conditions attached to it. So even if someone genuinely born again backslides into sin for the rest of their life, they're still going to heaven.

For someone who supposedly accepted Christ but now openly rejects Him or lives a lifestyle of sin, the Calvinist position is quite simple and tidy, "They were never saved in the first place." In other words, the person was not sincere when they first accepted Christ, and therefore they weren't truly born again, despite having the appearance of such. But is this true? Someone who rejects Christ was never sincere in their initial believing upon Him?

As an example, take the case of Charles Templeton (1915-2001). He first professed his faith in Jesus Christ in 1936 when he asked Jesus Christ to come into his heart. He became a pastor and, with his family and some friends, founded the *Avenue Road Church of the Nazarene* in Toronto (the name has since changed). Shortly after this, he became an evangelist. In 1945 Templeton began ministering in meetings with Billy Graham. The same year he helped pioneer *Youth for Christ International*. In 1946 Charles Templeton travelled with Billy Graham around Europe in the Youth for Christ European evangelistic tour. Charles Templeton and Billy Graham were even roommates on this tour. In 1946, he was listed among those *best used of God* by the National Association of Evangelicals. But by 1956, just ten years later, he openly rejected Christ and professed to be an agnostic. Forty years later, in 1996, he wrote a book called, *Farewell to God: My Reasons for Rejecting the Christian Faith*.

No one would question the sincerity of Templeton's initial born-again experience. No one would question his spiritual growth and fruit born for two decades. But clearly, in the end, Charles Templeton chose to reject Christ.

We have three choices here:

1. He was never saved in the first place.

2. He was genuinely saved, chose to reject Christ, but God will give him a pass and he'll experience eternal life anyhow.

3. He was saved, chose to abandon and reject his faith in Jesus Christ, and consequently has forfeited his salvation and eternal life.

What are we to make of this? And it's not just Charles Templeton. Many of us know people who seemed to have had genuine born-again experiences with Christ, but later in life rejected Him, either by active rejection, a lifestyle of sin or passive indifference (lukewarmness). I have a pastor friend who knows someone with a very similar story as Templeton. You will never convince my friend that this man was never truly saved.

IS IT POSSIBLE FOR A BELIEVER TO ABANDON THEIR FAITH AND REJECT CHRIST?

If people have free will to accept Christ, don't they also have free will to later reject Him? One way to answer this question is to see if there are any scriptural warnings to Christians about

41

abandoning the faith, rejecting Christ or what is called *apostasy*. There would be absolutely no reason to warn believers against falling away or abandoning their faith if it wasn't possible to do so. I don't have to warn my wife Debby about walking a tightrope across Niagara Falls because it's simply not realistically possible for her to do such a thing. Such a warning would be laughable, totally meaningless. A warning only has gravitas and meaning if it warns against something that is realistically possible. Yet Jesus and the writers of the New Testament warned about true believers in Christ falling away from Him on multiple occasions.

2 Peter 1:10

*For if you practice these qualities **you will never fall**.*

This shows the real possibility of a believer falling if they DON'T continue to practice those things.

John 16:1

*I have said all these things to you **to keep you from falling away**.*

Jesus was talking to His followers here. You can't fall away or defect from something you weren't first part of in the first place. A North Korean athlete couldn't defect to the United States if he or she wasn't a citizen of North Korea in the first place. Such a statement from Jesus shows falling away is possible for His followers. When Jesus taught about the end times, He focused on the danger of believers falling away because of hard times and persecution.

Matthew 24:9-12

9   *Then they will deliver you up to tribulation and put you to death, and you will be hated by all nations for my name's sake.*

10   *And then **many will fall away** and betray one another and hate one another.*

11   *And many false prophets will arise **and lead many astray**.*

12   *And because lawlessness will be increased, **the love of many will grow cold.***

Jesus taught that in the end times, when faced with persecution, many of His followers will fall away, be led astray, and whose love would grow cold. And He didn't say this would happen to a few, but to **many**. I believe today we are seeing the fulfillment of this before our very eyes.

In the parable of the sower and the seed in Luke 8, in explaining the parable to His disciples, Jesus showed that believers falling away is certainly possible.

Luke 8:13

*The seeds on the rocky soil represent those who **hear the message** and **receive it with joy**. But since they don't have deep roots, **they believe for a while**, then they **fall away** when they face temptation. (NLT)*

These people:
1. Heard the Word of God preached.
2. Believed the message.
3. Received the message.
4. Eventually fell away.

A straightforward reading of this verse would clearly indicate these people were saved. Jesus said *they believe for a while, then they **fall away**.* That same Greek word for *fall away* here in Luke is used by the Apostle Paul in 1 Timothy 4:1.

1 Timothy 4:1

*But the Spirit explicitly says that in later times some will **fall away from the faith**, paying attention to deceitful spirits and doctrines of demons. (NASB)*

You cannot *fall away* from something you weren't first part of! So this is talking about genuine believers who fall way from the faith they first embraced. One can try to make the case that they really weren't saved in the first place, but I believe that just doesn't make sense and is contrary to the plain reading and meaning of the verse.

1 Corinthians 10:12

*Therefore let anyone who thinks that he stands take heed **lest he fall.***

This warning only means something if it could realistically happen.

Hebrews 3:12

*Take care, brothers, lest there be in any of you an evil, unbelieving heart, leading you to **fall away** from the living God.*

You couldn't *fall away* from the living God unless you were first believing in the living God! And the author of Hebrews is talking to Christians here (*Take care, **brothers**)! A plain reading of Scripture makes it clear that it is possible for believers to fall away from God and abandon their faith.

1 Timothy 1:19

***Holding on to faith** and a good conscience, which some have rejected and so have suffered **shipwreck with regard to the faith**. (NLT)*

Why would we be exhorted to hold on to faith if believers were going to naturally and automatically persevere in faith to the very end anyhow (the Calvinist position)? This shows it's possible NOT to hold on to faith, and in doing so, suffer *shipwreck with regard to the faith*. A shipwrecked faith is a faith that has been rejected. And the Apostle Paul said this isn't theoretical, it actually happened to some people, saying, *which some have rejected*, referring to *their faith and a good conscience*. It's clear from this verse that it's possible to reject faith having once held onto it.

2 Thessalonians 2:3

*Let no one in any way deceive you, for it (the second coming of Christ) will not come unless the **apostasy (ESV/NIV – rebellion) comes first**, and the man of lawlessness is revealed, the son of destruction. (NASB)*

The Apostle Paul taught that one of the signs of the end times is that a great apostasy, or falling away, will come. There's been apostasy happening for two thousand years, but when Paul identifies the last days with "the apostasy," it's referring to apostasy on an exponentially and dramatically larger scale. The Greek word is *apostasia* means forsaking, falling away or defection. You can't fall away from something you weren't first part of! The same word, *apostasia*, is used in Acts 21:21. Here James and the leaders of the Jerusalem church responded to Paul's testimony of how God was moving in bringing Gentiles to faith in Christ.

Acts 21:21

And they have been told about you that you teach all the Jews who are among the Gentiles to forsake (apostasia, NLT -turn their backs on) Moses, telling them not to circumcise their children or walk according to our customs.

Obviously, the Jews could not have been accused of forsaking Moses unless they were first adhering to Moses. Back to 2 Thessalonians 2:3 (the second coming will not come unless the great apostasy comes first).

One prominent and well-respected biblical scholar makes two points about this which I believe to be wrong. First, that the faith which was abandoned here, was not a true faith, but a superficial and therefore not genuine faith. But the verse doesn't specify this qualification so I reject that out of hand. Second, he says this group of people who apostatized (verse 3) is the same group talked about in verse 10 where it says: *and with all wicked deception (talking about the coming deception of the anti-Christ in the last days) for those who are perishing, because they refused to love the truth and so be saved.* This scholar says verse 10 is clearly talking about people who were deceived, perishing and not saved, i.e., never saved. True, but it's a different group of people being talked about here than those in verse 3! People in verse 3 loved the truth at one time or else they couldn't fall away from it. To say it's the same group of people is trying to insert something that just isn't there. Verse 12 talks about those *who did not believe the truth but had pleasure in unrighteousness.* "Did not believe the truth" is past tense. The ones guilty of apostasy in verse 3 DID believe the truth and were saved at one time however. Verse 10 is talking about those who never believed in the first place. So the apostasy of verse 3 is those who had faith, then rejected faith afterwards. This means in the last days many believers will fall away from the faith. I've witnessed the reality of this many times over with people. And again, you can't fall away from something you were not first part of.

But there are more New Testament verses that clearly show that it's possible for genuine believers to choose later on to willfully reject their faith.

Hebrews 10:39

*But we are not of **those who shrink back** (turn away from God – NLT) and are destroyed, but of those who have faith and preserve their souls ("we are the faithful ones, whose souls will be saved" – NLT).*

The two choices here are shrink back to destruction (forfeiting one's salvation), or stay faithful to the saving of the soul. This verse only makes sense if it's possible for someone who once had faith, to shrink back and turn away from Christ.

Hebrews 6:4-6

4   *For it is impossible, in the case of those who have once been enlightened, who have tasted the heavenly gift, and have shared in the Holy Spirit,*

5   *and have tasted the goodness of the word of God and the powers of the age to come,*

6   ***and then have fallen away***, *to restore them again to repentance, since they are crucifying once again the Son of God to their own harm and holding him up to contempt.*

One would have to work very hard to explain away a plain reading of this passage. Look closely at the elements of this passage.

1. They were enlightened.
2. They had tasted of the heavenly gift (of salvation).
3. They shared in the Holy Spirit.
4. They tasted the goodness of the word of God.
5. They tasted the powers of the age to come.

If that doesn't describe true disciples of Christ, I don't know what does. Some people try to say these people weren't really born-again believers because it uses the word "tasted," which denotes that they didn't fully eat or experience the fullness of these things. Using that same logic, when it says in this same book, Hebrews 2:9, *"Jesus, crowned with glory and honor because of the suffering of death, so that by the grace of God **he might taste death for everyone**,"* we should assume Jesus didn't fully experience death. The argument fails immediately.

It clearly shows these people were saved and that it's possible for believers to fall away, forsake, defect or apostatize. And once doing so, it's impossible for them to repent and get back in right relationship with the Lord.

Romans 11:21-22

*For if God did not spare the natural branches, neither will he spare you. Note then the kindness and the severity of God: severity toward those who have fallen, but **God's kindness to you, provided you continue in his kindness. Otherwise you too will be cut off**.*

"Natural branches" here is referring to the Jews, the original receptors of God's promises and blessings. The word "you" is referring to the non-Jews or Gentiles, those who have been grafted into God's people. The Jews were cut off because of their rebellion, unbelief and rejection of Christ. But notice what the Apostle Paul says here about Christ-followers in the New Testament:

> "God's kindness to you, **provided** you
> continue in his kindness. Otherwise
> you too will be cut off."

"Provided" is conditional language. But what if one doesn't continue in His kindness? What if one rejects and forsakes God's kindness in Christ? The answer is clear, they too will be *cut off*, which speaks of God's rejection of them, preventing them from experiencing His salvation and eternal life. There are Christians, even biblical scholars, who believe people who were born again but didn't "continue in his kindness" will still be spared and not cut off. A plain reading of scripture indicates otherwise. Some will say this only applies to the larger group of Jews and Gentiles. It doesn't apply to individuals. Using that same logic, then only the larger group of Gentile believers are grafted in to being God's redeemed people now, not individuals. The argument falls apart and is just not valid.

At this point someone will bring up Romans 8:35 to make the point that nothing can separate us from the grace and love found in Jesus Christ. Therefore, they say, for those who are truly born again, they will experience eternal life no matter what. But carefully read the verse.

Romans 8:35

Who shall separate us from the love of Christ? Shall tribulation, or distress, or persecution, or famine, or nakedness, or danger, or sword?

I'll make two points about this. First, it doesn't say separate us from eternal life, it says separate us from the love of Christ. Even Christ's judgment at the very end of time will be an act of love for those sent to eternal punishment. Second, even if interpreting this as separating us from eternal life (which would be a wrong interpretation), note two things not mentioned in the list: 1) choosing to reject Christ and 2) living a continued lifestyle of sin, both of which would forfeit salvation.

Another verse people bring up to support the theology that a true believer can never forfeit that salvation is Philippians 1:6.

Philippians 1:6

And I am sure of this, that he who began a good work in you will bring it to completion at the day of Jesus Christ.

I'll make two important points on this verse.

First, there's nothing in the language here that makes this an unconditional guarantee. To read a guarantee into this verse is inserting something that's not there.

Second, the Apostle Paul is expressing his confidence that the Philippian believers will stay faithful to Christ. What is Paul's confidence based on? Just one verse prior tells us.

Philippians 1:5

*Because of your **partnership in the gospel from the first day until now.***

His confidence was based on these believers' continued faithfulness to walk with Christ! Additionally, this group of disciples supported Paul while he was in prison.

Philippians 1:7

It is right for me to feel this way about you all, because I hold you in my heart, for you are all partakers with me of grace, both in my imprisonment and in the defense and confirmation of the gospel.

Philippians 4:18

I have received full payment, and more. I am well supplied, having received from Epaphroditus the gifts you sent, a fragrant offering, a sacrifice acceptable and pleasing to God.

In Philippians 1:6, Paul was simply voicing his personal confidence in these disciples staying faithful to Christ based on their past track record. It wasn't a guarantee but a vote of confidence based on what he observed because of their faithfulness in following Christ.

But even this doesn't negate Paul from giving them a warning to imitate him and not those who have rejected Christ.

Philippians 3:17-19

Brothers, join in imitating me, and keep your eyes on those who walk according to the example you have in us. For many, of whom I have often told you and now tell you even with tears, walk as enemies of the cross of Christ. Their end is destruction, their god is their belly, and they glory in their shame, with minds set on earthly things.

Why the need for such a warning if their salvation was guaranteed?

He admonishes them to hang in there and keep on in their obedience, working out their salvation, and cooperating with God who is working in them.

Philippians 2:12-13

> *Therefore, my beloved, as you have always obeyed, so now, not only as in my presence but much more in my absence, **work out your own salvation with fear and trembling**, for it is **God who works in you**, both to will and to work for his good pleasure.*

Why would he say this if their salvation was a done deal...a guarantee? There would be not need! So to interpret Philippians 1:6 as a guarantee that believers can never turn away and reject Christ is a serious misinterpretation of the verse.

What happens when people, even believers, choose not to live for Christ anymore and instead, follow their fleshly, carnal desires? Let's look at two scriptures side-by-side.

Galatians 6:7-8	Romans 8:13
*Do not be deceived: God is not mocked, for whatever one sows, that will he also reap. For **the one who sows to his own flesh will from the flesh reap corruption**, but the one who sows to the Spirit will from the Spirit reap eternal life.*	*For **if you live according to the flesh you will die**, but if by the Spirit you put to death the deeds of the body, you will live.*

Keep in mind, in both cases, these verses are addressed to believers. The phrases "sows to his own flesh" and "live according to the flesh" indicate a believer's lifestyle of sin instead of surrendering to the reign of Christ and the Spirit. The result is "reap corruption" or "die," both phrases indicating the opposite of eternal life.

But what about Jude 1:24 that talks about the keeping power of God?

Jude 1:24

*Now to him who **is able to keep you from stumbling and to present you blameless** before the presence of his glory with great joy.*

People cite this verse to make the argument that no matter what a born-again believer does in this life, God will keep and guard them from stumbling so they ultimately receive eternal life. But keep this verse in context with what precedes it and with the rest of scripture. Earlier in the chapter it talks about scoffers in the last days with ungodly passions (vss 18-19). The admonition to believers comes next:

Jude 1:20-21

*But you, beloved, building yourselves up in your most holy faith and praying in the Holy Spirit, **keep yourselves in the love of God**, waiting for the mercy of our Lord Jesus Christ that leads to eternal life.*

Our part is to stay faithful...building ourselves up on our faith, praying, keeping ourselves in God's love and staying alert, waiting for His mercy. Believers staying faithful in verses 20 and 21 precedes being kept by God in verse 24. If this seems like a stretch, compare Jude 1:24 above with Colossians 1:22-23, which also talks about being presented blameless before Christ.

Colossians 1:22-23

*In order to present you holy and blameless and above reproach before him, **if** indeed you continue in the faith, stable and steadfast, not shifting from the hope of the gospel that you heard.*

The "presented blameless before His glory" of Jude 24 is the same "present you holy and blameless and above reproach before him" of Colossians 1:22-23. In both cases it's referring to the judgment seat of Christ (2 Corinthians 5:10), when we all stand before Him for judgment. Yes, he will "present us blameless before the presence of his glory" (Jude 1:24), IF INDEED we stay faithful and not shift or move away from the gospel! The promise, therefore, is conditional.

1 Peter 1:3-5

*He has caused us to be born again to a living hope through the resurrection of Jesus Christ from the dead, to an inheritance that is imperishable, undefiled, and unfading, kept in heaven for you, who by God's power are being guarded **through faith** for a salvation ready to be revealed in the last time.*

We see a number of key promises here:
- caused us to be born again
- to an inheritance imperishable
- kept in heaven for us
- guarded by God's power for salvation to be revealed in the last time

These are wonderful promises. But notice the condition to experiencing these promises, noted by the two critical words...***through faith***! We are guarded (Jude 24 – kept) by God's power through faith! This is in keeping with what we read in 1 John 2:24-24.

1 John 2:24-25

*Let what you heard from the beginning **abide in you**. If what you heard from the beginning **abides in you**, then you too will abide in the Son and in the Father. And this is the promise that he made to us—eternal life.*

Continuing to abide in Christ yields the result of eternal life, NOT saying the sinners' prayer X number of years ago, with no faithful following Christ afterwards.

Some point to Ephesians 4:30, stating that believers cannot forfeit salvation because they are sealed until the day of redemption. Let's look at this and make some observations.

Ephesians 4:30

*And do not grieve the Holy Spirit of God, by whom you were **sealed** for the day of redemption.*

The seal talked about here was a mark of ownership. And yes, when we accept Christ, God marks us as His own. 1 Corinthians 6:19-20 says, "You are not your own, for you were bought with a price." When we accepted Christ, the Holy Spirit was given to us as a seal that marked our ownership by God.

2 Corinthians 1:22

*Who has also put **his seal** on us and given us his Spirit in our hearts **as a guarantee.***

This translation (English Standard Version) is a little misleading when it uses the word "guarantee." The word isn't guarantee, it's "deposit" or "down payment." The NIV uses the word "deposit," the NLT says, "first installment," the NASB says, "as a pledge." There's a big difference between a deposit and a guarantee. As anyone knows, a deposit or down payment is NOT a guarantee, but is a sign of good faith, or *earnest*. The King James Version translates it, "given **the earnest** of the Spirit in our hearts." Earnest money is given as a down payment signifying serious intention. In one sense a deposit or down payment is a guarantee *assuming the conditions are met in the transaction*. But a down payment is not a guarantee if conditions are not met. It's like an engagement ring, which shows you're "now taken," a sign of serious intention, but in no way is it a guarantee if conditions aren't met.

Ephesians 1:13-14

*Were **sealed** with the promised Holy Spirit, who is the **guarantee** of our inheritance until we acquire possession of it, to the praise of his glory.*

I believe the translators took liberty here using the word "guarantee." The seal of the promised Spirit is not a guarantee, but a pledge or down payment for an inheritance yet to be fully received. The word "guarantee" means, "money which in purchases is given as a pledge or down payment that the full amount will subsequently be paid."[8] Again, a down payment or deposit is not a guarantee if conditions to the agreement are not met.

---

[8] Strong's #728 - *arrabōn*

Keep in mind, and this is critically important, that Ephesians 4:30 (*the Holy Spirit of God, by whom you were sealed for the day of redemption*) was written to a certain group of people who were abiding in Christ.

Ephesians 1:1

> To **the saints** who are in Ephesus, **and are faithful** in Christ Jesus:

This was whom the Holy Spirit was given to as a deposit for a future inheritance. It was given to those who had accepted Christ and **remained faithful** to Him.

Acts 5:32

> The Holy Spirit, whom God has given **to those who obey him.**

But there is nothing that says things can't change if conditions for eternal life don't continue to be met. A "seal" is not permanent by any means, just refer to: Daniel 12:9, Revelation 5:9, Revelation 6:1 and Revelation 20:3,7. In all cases, the seal was broken and unsealed by God Himself.

Again, there are numerous warnings in Scripture to continue and persevere in faith. Continuing and persevering is not assumed or guaranteed.

Acts 14:21-22

> They returned to Lystra and to Iconium and to Antioch, strengthening the souls of the disciples, **encouraging them to continue in the faith**, and saying that through many tribulations we must enter the kingdom of God.

Why would you have to exhort disciples to continue in the faith if it was assured anyhow?

The common thread in all of these passages is continuing in faith in Christ. It's not just one's initial faith expressed at an altar call years ago, it's an ongoing abiding in Christ.

Romans 1:17

*For in the gospel the righteousness of God is revealed—a righteousness that is **by faith from first to last**, just as it is written: "The righteous will live by faith." (NIV)*

It's "faith from first to last," that counts! That why Peter wrote:

1 Peter 1:9

*Obtaining **the outcome of your faith, the salvation of your souls.***

Add to this, passages that have a clear implication of someone who was once demonstrating fruit consistent with salvation, but then the nature of that relationship changes. For example:

Matthew 5:13

*You are the salt of the earth, but **if salt has lost its taste**, how shall its saltiness be restored? **It is no longer good for anything except to be thrown out** and trampled under people's feet.*

The salt was at one time "salty," but then something changed...it lost its saltiness. The result? It was thrown out. This could mean nothing but the loss of connection to God. If "thrown out" means something else, what?

2 Peter 3:17

*You therefore, beloved, knowing this beforehand, take care that you are not carried away **with the error of lawless people and lose** your own stability.*

This shows it's possible to be carried away into sin and lose stability in Christ. It is the opposite of Colossians 1:

Colossians 1:22-23

*In order to present you holy and blameless and above reproach before him, **if indeed you continue in the faith, stable and steadfast, not shifting from the hope of the gospel.***

Continuing in the faith is not guaranteed. It's a decision to stay faithful and not shift away from Christ.

1 Thessalonians 3:5

*For this reason, when I could bear it no longer, I sent **to learn about your faith**, for fear that somehow the tempter had tempted you and our labor would be in vain.*

Why would Paul be so concerned if it wasn't possible for these believers to reject their initial faith? Paul's concern was that they might slip off their initial faith and consequently all efforts for their salvation and eternal life would be in vain. We see Paul's concern for laboring in vain again with the Philippians.

Philippians 2:16

*You **shine as lights** in the world, **holding fast to the word of life**, so that in the day of Christ I may be proud that I did **not run in vain or labor in vain**.*

They shine as lights only when holding fast to the word of life. If they don't continue to hold fast, Paul's efforts would have been in vain.

It is possible for people who once believed in and followed God, to reject Him, even though He warns believers to continue in faith and hold fast.

Hebrews 12:25

*See that you **do not refuse him who is speaking**. For if they did not escape when they **refused him** who warned them on earth, much less will we escape **if we reject him** who warns from heaven.*

This warning shows clearly that believers can refuse and reject Christ. There are other scriptural examples of genuine believers eventually choosing to reject Christ and abandon their faith, but this chapter is not meant to be an exhaustive treatment of the subject. But let's move on and answer the second question, a question that is even more important...what is the fate of those who once genuinely accepted and followed Christ, but now reject Him by 1) open rejection, 2) living in sin 3) being lukewarm or by 4) embracing heresy?

Chapter 7

What is the Fate of Believers Who Fall Away?

By this time many people reading this will ask, "OK, genuine believers in Christ can fall away. But the real question is, what is their fate? Do they forfeit their salvation?"

Some will say they only forfeit their reward in heaven, not heaven itself. But is this true? Is scripture clear on what happens to those who abandon their faith?

Galatians 5:19-21

19 *Now the works of the flesh are evident: sexual immorality, impurity, sensuality,*

20 *idolatry, sorcery, enmity, strife, jealousy, fits of anger, rivalries, dissensions, divisions,*

21 *envy, drunkenness, orgies, and things like these. **I warn you, as I warned you before**, that **those who do such things will not inherit the kingdom of God**.*

Why would the Apostle Paul warn Christians about these works of sin if it wasn't possible for them to slip back into them and subsequently forfeit the kingdom of God? If the principle only applies to those not yet saved, why did Paul say, *I warn you, as I warned you before*? Why would he warn them twice if talking about an issue dealing with someone else? He's warning them because the warning applies to them, NOT the unregenerate! Some teachers try to make the point that Paul switches pronouns from *you* to *those*, meaning that he was talking about unsaved people, not the "saved" Galatians themselves. That logic doesn't work. If I was a high school football coach and admonished my team, "I warn you as I've warned you before, that those who break curfew and engage in drinking or similar things, will be kicked off the team," am I suddenly talking about players on a different team? No, I'm giving this warning to the team I'm talking to because it applies to them! Paul is warning believers here that those Christian Galatians who engage in a sinful lifestyle risk losing their inheritance of the kingdom of God. He wouldn't say it if it wasn't possible. Another verse from Galatians confirms this.

Galatians 6:8

> For the one who sows to his own flesh will from the flesh reap **corruption**, but the one who sows to the Spirit will from the Spirit reap eternal life.

The word "corruption" here is the Greek word, *phthora.* Thayer's Greek Lexicon states this word means, "destruction, perishing, loss of salvation."[9] Therefore in this verse, and keep in mind this is addressed to Christians, we have two choices: eternal life for those who continually sow to the Spirit, or loss of salvation for those who continually (as a lifestyle) sow to the flesh.

Some, no doubt, will quote John 14:16 in protest saying the Holy Spirit will be given to believers forever, and forever means forever.

John 14:16

> And I will ask the Father, and he will give you another Helper, to be with you forever.

But this is based on continuing to believe and follow Jesus Christ.

John 7:37-39

> 37 On the last day, the great day, of the feast, Jesus stood and cried aloud, "If anyone is thirsty, let him come to me and drink.

---

9 Corruption – Thayer's Greek Lexicon - https://www.blueletterbi-ble.org/lang/lexicon/lexicon.cfm?Strongs=G5356&t=KJV

38 **Whoever continues to believe in me will have,** as the
Scripture says, rivers of living water continuously flowing
from within him."

39 By this He referred to the Spirit that those believing in Him
were going to receive -- for the Spirit had not yet come,
because Jesus had not yet been glorified. (WNT)[10]

They'll also reference Matthew 28:20, making the same
point.

Matthew 28:20

And behold, **I am with you always,** to the end of the age.

But this is conditional upon continued abiding in Christ—
"Remain in me, and I will remain in you." John 15:4

Getting back to John 14:16 (the Holy Spirit will be with you
forever), we must keep this in context with Jesus' statements in
the same chapter.

John 14:21,23

Whoever has my commandments and keeps them, he it is who
loves me. And he who loves me will be loved by my Father, and
I will love him and manifest myself to him. ... If anyone loves me,
he will keep my word, and my Father will love him, and we will
come to him and make our home with him.

We see here that God's abiding presence is conditional upon
loving Him, and loving Him is clearly defined as keeping His Word,
which speaks of faithfulness in works of obedience.

The fate of believers who return to a lifestyle or practice of
sin, is to forfeit their inheritance of the kingdom of God and eternal
life.

2 Timothy 2:12

---

[10] Williams New Testament - http://studybible.info/Williams/John%207
– Here Charles B. Williams, in his translation, emphasizes the tense of
the verb to pull out its meaning.

If we endure, we will also reign with him; if we deny him, he also will deny us.

The "we" here is addressing believers, for Paul is not addressing concerns with unbelievers. And there are only two choices mentioned here, enduring or denying. Enduring results in reigning with Christ in heaven. But if we (believers) deny Christ, He will deny us. This shows it is possible to believe and accept Christ, but reject and deny Him later.

Some will quote the next verse, verse 13, to argue the point that even if we don't stay faithful to Christ, He will still stay faithful to the faithless, still granting them eternal life: *if we are faithless, he remains faithful—for he cannot deny himself.* But this doesn't mean He will give the faithless eternal life, it means that He will still be faithful to do what He said in His Word. And what did He said in His Word that He would do? *If we deny Him, He will deny us* (verse12).

Matthew 10:33

Whoever denies me before men, **I also will deny** *before my Father who is in heaven.*

This certainly does not mean they will be welcomed in heaven for eternal life after denying Him. Conversely, the promise that Jesus Christ will confess us before the Father at judgment is conditional.

Revelation 3:5

The one who conquers will be clothed thus in white garments, and I will never blot (erase – NASB) his name out of the book of life. I will confess his name before my Father and before his angels.

Pinging off both 2 Timothy 2:12 and Matthew 10:33, it's the one who conquers and endures that Christ will confess before the Father and angels at judgment.

What's even more telling in Revelation 3:5 are His words, *and I will never blot his name out of the book of life.* If it wasn't possible for a name to be erased from the book of life, this verse would be meaningless. This shows it's possible for a name once in the book of life to be taken out of it. Some try to say that every human being's name is written in the book of life when they're born, and only erased if they don't accept Christ. I don't think so. Notice what Paul says in Philippians 4:3.

Philippians 4:3

*Yes, I ask you also, true companion, help these women, who have labored side by side with me in the gospel together with Clement and the rest of my fellow workers, **whose names are in the book of life**.*

If every person born on earth had their name written in the book of life, there would be no need for Paul to say what he did. It's obvious here that those talked about here were faithful believers in Christ and therefore their names were written in the book of life. From Revelation 3:5 then, those believers who don't remain faithful to Christ, will have their names erased from the book of life. And what does that result in?

Revelation 20:15

*And if anyone's name was **not found written in the book of life**, he was thrown into the lake of fire.*

This is the fate of those who don't remain faithful followers of Jesus Christ, but instead fall away from Him. They don't get to experience the eternal reign of God.

John 8:51

*Truly, truly, I say to you, if anyone **keeps my word**, he will **never see death**.*

"Never sees death" = eternal life. "Keeps" is present tense. If one has a present tense saving faith, a faith which yields the fruit of keeping God's Word, they will never see death. Not physical death, but the second death, which is being thrown into the lake of fire (Revelation 20:14). For this verse to have real meaning, the opposite would have to be true. If one initially had faith but chooses a lifestyle of not keeping God's Word, they will see death, i.e., the second death. John 8:51 (if anyone keeps my word, he will never see death) is similar to 1 John 2:24-25

1 John 2:24-25

> **Let** what you heard from the beginning **abide in you**. If what you heard from the beginning **abides in you**, then you too will abide in the Son and in the Father. And this is the promise that he made to us—**eternal life**.

If what we have heard from the beginning (God's Word, the gospel of salvation) abides in us (we stay faithful to God), we have the promise of eternal life. But what if it doesn't? Then we don't have eternal life. And notice the word "let." "**Let** what you heard from the beginning abide in you." This means we have a choice.

These verses continue to show that salvation can be forfeited.

Luke 9:62

> "No one who puts his hand to the plow and looks back is fit for the kingdom of God."

"Puts his hand to the plow" indicates engagement in the kingdom of God. "Looks back" shows the possibility of choosing to be drawn away from the kingdom back into the world. The result of this is forfeiting their share in the kingdom of God.

Matthew 25:1-12

> 1 Then the kingdom of heaven will be like ten virgins who took their lamps and went to meet the bridegroom.
>
> 2 Five of them were foolish, and five were wise.
>
> 3 For when the foolish took their lamps, they took no oil with them,
>
> 4 but the wise took flasks of oil with their lamps.
>
> 5 As the bridegroom was delayed, they all became drowsy and slept.
>
> 6 But at midnight there was a cry, 'Here is the bridegroom! Come out to meet him.'

7   Then all those virgins rose and trimmed their lamps.

8   And the foolish said to the wise, 'Give us some of your oil, for our lamps are going out.'

9   But the wise answered, saying, 'Since there will not be enough for us and for you, go rather to the dealers and buy for yourselves.'

10 And while they were going to buy, the bridegroom came, and those who were ready went in with him to the marriage feast, and the door was shut.

11 Afterward the other virgins came also, saying, 'Lord, lord, open to us.'

12 But he answered, 'Truly, I say to you, I do not know you.'

We need to get this straight, all ten virgins here were Christians. The five foolish virgins were part of the wedding party awaiting the groom's appearance! All ten virgins believed in the bridegroom. All ten virgins looked forward to the marriage feast. But only five gained entrance. The other five were foolish, got distracted by other things and were not prepared when the bridegroom came. They didn't stay faithful and alert. What was the result? They were not allowed into the marriage feast, the bridegroom responding to their pleads of "Lord, Lord" with, "I do not know you." This sounds very similar to Matthew 7:21-23 when they also cried out, "Lord, Lord," but Christ responded, "I never knew you, depart from Me." The point here—only those who stay faithful, alert and prepared are allowed to enter "the marriage supper of the Lamb," (Revelation 19:6-9).

So what is the fate of believers who sometime, after receiving Christ, reject Him?

Hebrews 10:26-31

26 For **if we go on sinning deliberately after** receiving the knowledge of the truth, there no longer remains a sacrifice for sins,

²⁷ but **a fearful expectation of judgment, and a fury of fire** that will consume the adversaries.

²⁸ Anyone who has set aside the law of Moses dies without mercy on the evidence of two or three witnesses.

²⁹ How much worse punishment, do you think, will be deserved by **the one who has trampled underfoot the Son of God**, and has profaned the blood of the covenant by which he was sanctified, and has outraged the Spirit of grace?

³⁰ For we know him who said, "**Vengeance** is mine; I **will repay**." And again, "**The Lord will judge his people**."

³¹ It is a fearful thing to fall **into the hands of the living God**.

This is talking about Christians (the author uses the word "we") who, after receiving Christ, deliberately go back into a lifestyle of sin. "Falling into the hands of the living God" shows they were in His hand. It even says, "The Lord will judge <u>His</u> people," indicating exactly who this passage is referring to. But what is the result of believers who fall away from Christ?

- A fearful expectation of judgment.
- A fury of fire that will consume.
- Death without mercy.
- The vengeance (repaying) of God.

You would have to work very hard to convince me this is not talking about believers who have apostatized (fallen away). You'd have to pull off some amazing hermeneutical *sleight of hand* to explain away these verses as pertaining to unbelievers, not believers. These people went on deliberately sinning *AFTER RECEIVING the knowledge of the truth* (verse 26). The passage is in reference to *his people* (verse 30), those *in the hands of the living God* (verse 31). A plain reading shows that it is talking about Christians who have fallen away. What can they expect? The answer...*a fearful expectation of judgment, a fury of fire that will consume* them.

2 Peter 2:20-22

20   For if, after they have escaped the defilements of the world through the knowledge of our Lord and Savior Jesus Christ, they are again entangled in them and overcome, **the last state has become worse for them than the first.**

21   For it would have been better for them never to have known the way of righteousness than **after knowing it to turn back** from the holy commandment delivered to them.

22   What the true proverb says has happened to them: "The dog returns to its own vomit, and the sow, after washing herself, returns to wallow in the mire."

A careful reading will show that the people being talked about here were Christian believers who fell away and backslid into sin. They escaped the defilements of the world but then went back to them and became entangled in sin once again. And what is their fate? Their future, their eternity is worse than if they had never accepted Christ in the first place. Why? Because they tasted of Christ, they experienced *the knowledge of our Lord and Savior Jesus Christ* (verse 20), they experienced *the way of righteousness* (verse 21), but then turned away and became *again entangled* in the defilement of sin (verse 20). The result is even more of a severe judgment than someone who had never known Christ.

Romans 8:13

For if you live according to the flesh you will die, but if by the Spirit you put to death the deeds of the body, you will live.

The Apostle Paul is addressing Christians here and tells them that if they live according to the flesh they will die. Living "according to the flesh" is living with an absence of surrender to Christ. It is a life that follows the dictates of the world, flesh and the devil. The result is death. This couldn't mean physical death because even believers who live holy lives will experience that. No, this is referring to "the second death" mentioned in the book of Revelation.

Revelation 20:14

Then Death and Hades were thrown into the lake of fire. This is **the second death,** *the lake of fire.*

If one rejects the reign of God over their lives and chooses to live according to the flesh, a life not surrendered to Christ, this is what awaits them. And again, this verse (Romans 8:13), was addressed to the Christian believers in Rome.

What is the fate of those believers who don't remain in and stay faithful to Jesus Christ? Let's closely look at the words of Jesus Himself.

John 15:1-6

1   *I am the true vine, and my Father is the vinedresser.*

2   ***Every branch in me that does not bear fruit he takes away,*** *and every branch that does bear fruit he prunes, that it may bear more fruit.*

3   *Already you are clean because of the word that I have spoken to you.*

4   *Abide in me, and I in you. As the branch cannot bear fruit by itself, unless it abides in the vine, neither can you, unless you abide in me.*

5   *I am the vine; you are the branches. Whoever abides in me and I in him, he it is that bears much fruit, for apart from me you can do nothing.*

6   ***If anyone does not abide in me he is thrown away*** *like a branch and withers; and the branches are gathered,* ***thrown into the fire, and burned.***

Verse 2:   Every branch <u>in me</u> that does not bear fruit <u>he takes away</u>.

Verse 6:   If anyone does not abide in me he is thrown away like a branch and withers; and the branches are gathered, thrown into the fire, and burned.

The metaphor is branches connected to the vine. The vine is Jesus, the branches are believers. The branches that were connected to the vine at one time but don't remain faithful to grow and produce fruit are taken away and thrown into the fire. We're reminded of what we read earlier in Hebrews 10:27, *a fearful expectation of judgment, and a fury of fire.*

The key to avoiding this horrible consequence is this all-important word, *abide.* It is the Greek word *menō,* and means, "to remain, to dwell and continue in." It also means "endure," see John 6:27 (*the food that endures to eternal life*) and 1 Peter 1:25 (*but the word of the Lord endures forever* – NIV). If we, as branches, remain and continue in the Vine (Christ), if we endure in our worship, love, service and trust in Him, we will bear fruit. If not, the branches cut off and thrown away into the fire.

But what about verses that indicate that believers can't forfeit eternal life? A passage usually cited for this is found in John 10.

John 10:27-29

27 *My sheep **hear** my voice, and I know them, and they **follow** me.*

28 ***I give them eternal life, and they will never perish, and no one will snatch them out of my hand.***

29 *My Father, who has given them to me, is greater than all, and **no one is able to snatch them out of the Father's hand.***

Three critical points need to be made here.

1. It doesn't say this promise is unconditional. To read the promise as unconditional is to posit something that's just not there. If anything, the promise is conditional (refer to point 3).

2. "No one" here means other people, not the person him or herself. No one has the power to force you to fall or turn away from Jesus Christ. But—scripture states in many places that people can individually choose to reject Christ after first following Him. Remember earlier, Hebrews 6:4-6: "For it is impossible, in the case of those who have once been enlightened, who have tasted the

heavenly gift ... *and then have fallen away*, to restore them again to repentance." Does John 10:27-29 and Hebrews 6:4-6 contradiction each other? No. John 10 is saying no other people can snatch believers out of Jesus' hand.

The Greek word "snatch" here, *harpazō*, is the same word used in 1 Thessalonians 4:17, where it talks about either the rapture or the second coming, depending on your theology, when we shall be "caught up together with them in the clouds to meet the Lord in the air." In that event, *harpazō* means an action forcefully caused by another person, in this case Jesus Christ, coming for His church. *Harpazō* is connected to another person, not the person themselves. In John 10:28, *no one is able to snatch them out of the Father's hand*, means the same thing...no outside person or being, not another human and not the devil, is able for forcefully snatch them out of the Lord's hand. However, this doesn't rule out the real possibility of the person themselves choosing to reject Christ and discontinue following Him. One just needs to read Hebrews 10:38-39 to see this reality.

Hebrews 10:38-39

*My righteous one shall live by faith, and **if he shrinks back**, my soul has no pleasure in him. But we are not of **those who shrink back and are destroyed**, but of those who have faith and preserve their souls.*

We preserve our souls through continued faith, but it is possible to shrink back from God, resulting in destruction.

3. The verbs in verse 27; *hear* and *follow*, are Greek verbs in the present active indicative tense, which generally speaks of present and ongoing action. The meaning here should be obvious...as long as a sheep continues to *hear* and *follow* the Shepherd, no one can snatch them out of His hand, and He gives them eternal life. This is confirmed by numerous scriptures.

Revelation 2:10

Be faithful unto death, and I will give you the crown of life.

John 6:37

All that the Father gives me will come to me, and whoever comes to me I will never cast out.

The context surrounding this verse in John 6 is Jews struggling to understand that Jesus is the promised Messiah sent from God. The verse simply says that those Jews (or non-Jews for that matter) who come to Jesus and accept Him as Messiah, He will accept and in no way reject. The verse doesn't not speak to unconditional eternal security, and to read that into the verse is an unfortunate error.

FORFEITING ETERNAL LIFE BY COMPLACENCY

This poses another question—what about those who were genuinely born again, but haven't rejected Christ or backslidden into a lifestyle of sin, but they no longer faithfully are actively engaged in following Christ? In other words, what about those who have settled into a life of complacency in regards to following Christ, not actively following Him? We will let Jesus answer this question.

Revelation 3:15-16

*I know your works: you are neither cold nor hot. Would that you were either cold or hot! So, **because you are lukewarm, and neither hot nor cold, I will spit you out of my mouth.***

Jesus' preference is that we're either in or out, cold or hot. His will is that we be hot.

Romans 12:11

*Do not be slothful in zeal, be **fervent** in spirit, serve the Lord.*

The word "fervent" here in the Greek language means, "to be hot." Here's the Amplified Bible Classic Edition, which brings out the Greek nuance of "zeal.":

*Never lag in zeal and in earnest endeavor; be **aglow and burning with the Spirit**, serving the Lord.*

God prefers people on fire, hot. If they can't be hot, He prefers them cold. This means never having accepted Him in the first place. This is very similar to what was said earlier in 2 Peter 2:21, "For it would have been better for them never to have known the way of righteousness than after knowing it to turn back from the holy commandment delivered to them."

What is not acceptable to Jesus is being lukewarm. Lukewarm is the place of complacency and status quo, neither hot nor cold. Lukewarm is a little bit of hot with a little bit of cold. People in this condition will be spit out of Jesus' mouth, leaving them poised for destruction unless they change.

Proverbs 1:32

*For the simple are killed by their turning away, and **the complacency of fools destroys them**.*

Lukewarmness and complacency have consequences.

FOUR WAYS OF FORFEITING SALVATION

Eternal life, once possessed, can be forfeited through four possible scenarios:

1. Backsliding into a lifestyle of sin.

    - At a certain point of time of living in sin once having received Christ, living in sin becomes tantamount to declaring Jesus Christ is no longer Lord over one's life. I can't say what that point is. No one can but God alone. But in light of Matthew 7:15-20 (you'll recognize them by their fruits, which we will get to in Chapter 11), we can certainly discern someone is at risk and try to save their life by leading them back to repentance and discipleship.

2 Timothy 2:25-26

Correcting his opponents with gentleness. God may perhaps grant them repentance leading to a knowledge of the truth, and they may come to their senses and escape from the snare of the devil, after being captured by him to do his will.

Jude 1:23

Save others by snatching them out of the fire.

. 2.   Choosing to reject Christ and not believe in Him any longer.

- I have already adequately shown that willfully rejecting Christ and forfeiting salvation is possible.

3.   Living a lukewarm life, neither hot nor cold.

- As we've seen from Revelation 3:15-16, living a lukewarm lifestyle results in Jesus spitting one out of His mouth. This can mean none other than forfeiting eternal life.

4.   False, heretical doctrine.

- Heretical doctrine that contradicts the orthodox tenets of faith of Christianity results in forfeiting one's eternal destiny.

2 Peter 2:1

*But false prophets also arose among the people, just as there will be false teachers among you, who will secretly bring in **destructive heresies**, even denying the Master who bought them, **bringing upon themselves swift destruction**.*

Galatians 1:6-9

*I am astonished that you are so quickly deserting him who called you in the grace of Christ and are turning to **a different gospel**—not that there is another one, but there are some who trouble you and want to distort the gospel of Christ. But even if we or an angel from heaven should preach to you a gospel contrary to the one we preached to you, **let him be accursed**. As we have said before, so now I say again: If anyone is preaching to you a gospel contrary to the one you received, let him be accursed.*

Revelation 22:19

If anyone takes away from the words of the book of this prophecy, God will take away his share in the tree of life and in the holy city, which are described in this book.

It's important for me to again stress that salvation is by grace alone through faith alone. One didn't gain salvation by good works, but by acknowledging, receiving and following Jesus Christ. One doesn't forfeit salvation by bad works, but by rejection of Jesus Christ. But again, at a certain point, living in sin or lukewarmness becomes the equivalent of rejecting Christ and His rulership over one's life.

TWO TYPES OF 'WORKS'

Here we must discern between two types of good works.

1. Works meant to earn salvation.

Scripture is very clear that we cannot earn God's favor or salvation by good works intended to secure eternal life.

Galatians 2:16

We know that a person is not justified by works of the law but through faith in Jesus Christ, so we also have believed in Christ Jesus, in order to be justified by faith in Christ and not by works of the law, because by works of the law no one will be justified.

Ephesians 2:8-9

For by grace you have been saved through faith. And this is not your own doing; it is the gift of God, not a result of works, so that no one may boast.

The fuel that motivates someone for this category of works is to gain God's favor and be granted salvation. Hebrews 6:1 calls this category of works, "dead works" because they are ineffective and produce nothing.

2. Works resulting from salvation.

The second kind of works in Scripture are good works that are **a result of** being saved and becoming a "new creation in Christ," 2 Corinthians 5:17. These good works result from faith in Christ and subsequent transformation in the discipleship process.

Ephesians 2:10

*For we are his workmanship, **created in Christ Jesus for good works**, which God prepared beforehand, that we should walk in them.*

Noticing the order here, we experience being "in Christ Jesus" and the Spirit's work in our hearts **first**, then we walk in the resulting good works that spring from that. Good works are the *fruit* of salvation, not the *root* of salvation.

The fuel that motivates someone for this category of works is a changed life by the power of the Holy Spirit. This does not happen automatically however; our will and choices are still involved. Even though an athlete, through training, has the power and ability to perform a certain action, he or she must still decide to take that action. Having the ability does not guarantee an action will be taken. This leads us to the Book of James.

Chapter 8

James and the Nature of Faith

CAN THAT FAITH SAVE HIM?

Many Christians, in fact most Christians, have a hard time reconciling what the Apostle James said in his letter with what the Apostle Paul said in his letters.

Paul: It's faith alone.
James: It's not faith alone.

It's not hard to reconcile the two if one knows **what kind of faith** James is referring to in James 2.

James 2:14-17

14 What good is it, my brothers, if someone says he has faith but does not have works? Can that faith save him?

15 If a brother or sister is poorly clothed and lacking in daily food,

16 and one of you says to them, "Go in peace, be warmed and filled," without giving them the things needed for the body, what good is that?

17 So also faith by itself, if it does not have works, is dead.

Here we have to define two terms, *works* and *faith*. The works that James refers to in James 2 are works that spring from a genuine faith experienced from a sincere salvation or regeneration experience. These works are category 2 works mentioned earlier, works not meant to earn God's favor, but resulting from salvation and empowered by the Spirit.

James asks a critical question here in verse 14, "Can that faith save him?" Young's Literal translation reads, "Is that faith able to save him?" In grammar, the word "that" is a definite article, referring to something specific that follows. "Can that faith save him?" refers to a specific kind of faith. What kind of faith? The answer according to James is... the kind that has no corresponding works! If that kind of faith has no corresponding works, it's a "dead" faith, a false faith, a deceived faith, or minimally, a disobedient faith.

James says in verse 17, "So also faith by itself, if it does not have works, is dead." Faith that does not have corresponding works of obedience is a dead faith, a faith that is lifeless.

James 2:18

*But someone will say, "You have faith and I have works." **Show me your faith** apart from your works, and **I will show you my faith** by my works.*

The point here is that you can't have one without the other! Genuine salvation faith is expressed by works of obedience. The word "show" (**"Show** me your faith" and "I will **show** you my faith") indicates that faith must be visible through works or actions of faithfulness. I believe this aligns perfectly with 1 Timothy 4:15.

1 Timothy 4:15

*Practice these things, immerse yourself in them, **so that all may see your progress**.*

Visible progress (fruit) is important. The typical American mindset is, "My progress is between me and God!" The Apostle Paul would disagree. A faith that has no visible works of obedience is a dead faith.

James 2:19

You believe that God is one; you do well. Even the demons believe—and shudder!

James stresses the point that even the devil and demons believe in God...therefore belief by itself gains nothing. For someone to claim, "I believe in Jesus therefore I'm saved," has about as much weight as the devil believing in Jesus and therefore is saved.

James 2:20-23

20   *Do you want to be shown, you foolish person, that faith apart from works is useless?*

21   *Was not Abraham our father justified by works when he offered up his son Isaac on the altar?*

22   *You see that faith was active along with his works, and faith was completed by his works;*

23   *and the Scripture was fulfilled that says, "Abraham believed God, and it was counted to him as righteousness"—and he was called a friend of God.*

To prove believing in Christ without faithful works of obedience is ineffective or inactive, James references Abraham: *Was not Abraham our father justified by works when he offered up his son Isaac on the altar?* Abraham was justified by works? Wait just a minute! Genesis 15:6 says, *And he believed the Lord, and he counted it to him as righteousness.* And Romans 4:9 confirms this, *For we say that faith was counted to Abraham as righteousness.* It's quoted again here in James 2:23. Scripture says it was Abraham's faith that was counted to him as righteousness, but James said, *Was not Abraham our father justified by works when he offered up his son Isaac on the altar?* How can this be? The answer—because faith must be coupled with works or it is not the kind of faith that saves!

Still speaking of Abraham, Verse 22 says, *faith was completed by his works.* We complete faith with corresponding works. A faith without works is incomplete.

> A faith that saves is a faith that obeys.

Keep in mind the kind of works we're talking about here...NOT the kind that earns us favor with God, but the kind that springs from regeneration (being born again) and empowered by the Spirit.

And then we come to a most startling statement by James.

James 2:24

You see that a person is justified by works and not by faith alone.

Put this verse on your church sign and see how it goes. By morning it will be riddled with bullets from gun-toting Calvinists! I posted this verse all by itself, no commentary, on FaceBook one time. One longtime Christian responded, "Not!" I thought, "Not?" Did "Not!" mean that James was in error? Did "Not!" mean James said it but I don't agree with it?

But think about what this is saying. If we survey the great faith hall of fame in Hebrews 11, we find something interesting.

Hebrews 11
4   By faith Abel offered a more acceptable sacrifice
7   By faith Noah constructed an Ark
8   By faith Abraham left his home and travelled to the land of promise
17 By faith, when he was tested, offered up Isaac
20 By faith Isaac blessed Jacob and Esau
21 By faith Jacob blessed the sons of Joseph
22 By faith Joseph spoke about the exodus of Israel from Egypt
23 By faith Moses' parents hid him
24 By faith Moses refused to be called the son of Pharaoh's daughter
28 By faith Moses kept the Passover and sprinkled the blood
29 By faith the Israelites crossed the Red Sea on dry land
30 By faith the walls of Jericho fell down as they shouted
31 By faith Rahab gave a friendly welcome to the spies

These all acted in faith. But how do we know? We know because they all had corresponding actions that expressed faith. Every one of these people demonstrated their faith by an action taken. This is exactly what James is pointing out—that true faith has corresponding actions or works.

You see that a person is justified by works and not by faith alone.

James is saying that the kind of faith that justifies is a faith that is coupled with works that express belief. If that faith doesn't express itself in works of obedience and faithfulness, it is not real faith, it is simply intellectual credence, or mental assent. James 2:25 asks a question:

James 2:25

And in the same way was not also Rahab the prostitute justified by works when she received the messengers and sent them out by another way?

Rahab's faith became visible only by her works. Her works completed, or brought to completion, her faith. James 2:22, *faith was completed by his (Abraham's) works.* Faith and works go hand-in-hand. Biblical faith is not divorced from works of faithfulness and obedience.

> It's the faith and not faith's works which saves us, but true faith will express itself in works.

In other words, we're justified by the kind of genuine faith that expresses itself in works. No expression of works means no genuine faith. This passage in James ends with verse 26.

James 2:26

For as the body apart from the spirit is dead, so also faith apart from works is dead.

Faith that is void of faithful works of obedience is a dead faith, and dead faith does NOT result in salvation or eternal life. It's *profession* without *possession.* And remember what Jesus said about those who profess but who do not have faithful works of obedience.

Matthew 7:21-23

*Not everyone who says to me, "Lord, Lord," will enter the kingdom of heaven, **but the one who does the will of my***

> **Father** *who is in heaven. On that day many will say to me,*
> *"Lord, Lord, did we not prophesy in your name, and cast out*
> *demons in your name, and do many mighty works in your*
> *name?" And then will I declare to them, "I never knew*
> *you; depart from me,* **you workers of lawlessness."**

Workers of lawlessness do not enter heaven, even if they professed Christ at one point. The ones who enter heaven are those possessing true, genuine and sincere faith (trust) coupled with a lifestyle that manifests that faith through discipleship and works of obedience.

Chapter 9

The Nature of Salvation

Eternal life is conditional, that condition including elements we've listed before: *repent, believe, receive* and *follow*. If someone chooses to reject engagement with these things, the condition for eternal life has not continued to be met. This doesn't mean we express these elements in our own, self-generated power. The last chapter of this book will touch on that. But when someone chooses to no longer believe upon and follow Jesus Christ, the condition for eternal life is no longer being met. Even if a person had initial faith, but rejected Christ later, they have forfeited eternal life, for they have forfeited the conditions.

I find it interesting that the same Greek word *faith* (*pistis*) is also translated *faithfulness* in Galatians 5:22. One time it's translated "faith," one time translated "faithfulness."

Hebrews 6:1

*Not laying again a foundation of repentance from dead works and of **faith** (pistis) toward God.*

Galatians 5:22

*But the fruit of the Spirit is love, joy, peace, patience, kindness, goodness, **faithfulness** (pistis).*

Faith and remaining faithful go hand-in-hand. *Faith* begins the journey, *faithfulness* completes it. Advocates of OSAS do not factor in the scriptural conditions of <u>continued</u> believing and faithfulness.

Revelation 17:14

*He is Lord of lords and King of kings, and those **with him** are called and chosen and **faithful**.*

Revelation 2:10

*Be **faithful unto death**, and I will give you the crown of life.*

Eternal life is conditional upon staying faithful and enduring. Not enduring, not staying faithful to Christ forfeits the crown of (eternal) life.

Matthew 24:13

*But the one who **endures to the end will be saved**.*

This is talking about faithfulness in maintaining our love for God. Just look at the previous verse, verse 12—*And because lawlessness will be increased, the love of many will grow cold*. Verse 12 is talking about people's love for God growing cold, which is a mark of the last days. Those who endure, those who faithfully continue to love God to the end will be saved. What's implicit in the verse is...those who don't endure to the end, won't be saved. If those who don't endure to the end are still saved, the verse becomes meaningless. Luke's account reads this way:

Luke 21:18-19

*But not a hair of your head will perish. **By your endurance you will gain your lives**.*

"But not a hair of your head will perish," is not talking about physically, for just two verses prior, verse 16, it says, *some of you they will put to death*. This is talking about spiritually, gaining eternal life. And it says, "By your endurance you will gain your lives." Eternal life is forfeited by not enduring, but is gained by faithfulness to Christ to the very end.

Revelation 3:10

Because you have kept my word about patient endurance, *I will keep you from the hour of trial that is coming on the whole world, to try those who dwell on the earth.*

Note the conditional language in that verse: "Because you have ... I will ..." This drives Calvinists crazy because their position is that the experience of eternal life is not connected to anything humans have done or will do. This verse says otherwise.

ETERNAL LIFE IS IN THE SON

Something that is helpful here, is an understanding of where eternal life is, that is, where it is found.

1 John 5:12

Whoever has the Son has life; whoever does not have the Son of God does not have life.

Eternal life is not found in any of us, it is only found in Jesus Christ. If you "have" the Son (not *had* the Son), you have eternal life. But if you do not have the Son, you do not have eternal life.

"Has" here is in the present tense, not past tense: *Whoever has the Son has life*. The present tense generally indicates present and usually continuous action. If you are presently and faithfully believing and following Jesus Christ, you have eternal life. If not, you don't. If someone willfully rejects the Son, they reject and forfeit eternal life. "Continuing" is the key. God's will is that those who accept Christ *continue*.

John 9:31

If you abide (continue – NASB) in my word, you are truly my disciples.

The implicit truth in this verse is, if you don't abide and continue in His word, you are not His disciples.

THE NATURE OF SALVATION

A broader understanding of salvation will help our understanding with this subject. The *once saved always saved* proponents advocate for the position that once believing and receiving Christ, one is saved, and salvation at that point is a done

85

deal, it can't be lost or undone—nothing to see here so move along. But is that true?

As we look very carefully a scripture, we see that salvation has a past, present and future component to it. The journey begins the moment we accept Christ. The journey of salvation continues in the present. The journey of salvation finds its completion at the very end, at the second coming of Christ and the day of Judgment when entrance into the eternal state is gained or denied.

The best way to frame the journey is: *I was saved and am continuing to be saved, and hoping in the completion of my salvation.*

Some will recoil with this idea of hoping for a future salvation, but Scripture affirms a future hope of salvation. And why would you hope for something you possessed guaranteed in the present?

1 Thessalonians 5:8

*But since we belong to the day, let us be sober, having put on the breastplate of faith and love, and for a helmet **the hope of salvation.***

Romans 8:23-24

*As we wait eagerly for our adoption to sonship, the redemption of our bodies. For **in this hope we were saved.** But hope that is seen is no hope at all. **Who hopes for what they already have?***

I thought when we accepted Christ we were already adopted into God's family as sons and daughters! We did, it started then, but we hope for its completion at the second coming of Christ. And so our hope is in the completion of the salvation journey when we experience heaven. The truth is, salvation is a journey, a process we are currently in.

1 Corinthians 1:18

*For the word of the cross is folly to those who are perishing, but to us **who are being saved** it is the power of God.*

Salvation is past, present and future.

Past - Justification

The past aspect of our salvation is justification. Justification is the act of justifying someone so that they are no longer guilty. Those who respond to God's initiation and overtures of grace and become genuinely born again, are declared justified or righteous through what Jesus Christ did for us on the cross. There is a God part and a man part. God's part is moving upon man's heart by drawing them to the reality of God. In grace, God touches and opens their heart to see and understand the gospel.

Acts 16:14

The Lord opened her (Lydia's) heart to pay attention to what was said by Paul.

Man's part is responding to God's invitation by saying 'yes.'

Acts 16:15

And after she was baptized...

This shows Lydia responded to God's invitation. After receiving Christ, we are justified in God's sight. Justification is a legal granting of being in right-standing with God. In that sense, we were saved at the time we responded to and accepted Christ.

Romans 8:24

*For in this hope **we were** saved.*

Ephesians 2:5

*Even when we were dead in our trespasses, made us alive together with Christ—by grace you **have been saved**.*

Ephesians 2:8

*For by grace you **have been saved** through faith.*

2 Timothy 1:9

Who saved us and called us to a holy calling, not because of our works but because of his own purpose and grace, which he gave us in Christ Jesus before the ages began.

Titus 3:5

He saved us, not because of works done by us in righteousness, but according to his own mercy, by the washing of regeneration and renewal of the Holy Spirit.

Present - Sanctification

The present aspect of salvation is sanctification, which is the work of the Holy Spirit by which believers are progressively transformed into the image of Christ and walk in holiness.

2 Corinthians 3:18

*And we all, with unveiled face, beholding the glory of the Lord, **are being transformed** into the same image from one degree of glory to another. For this comes from the Lord who is the Spirit.*

Sanctification is the process that involves believers increasingly being empowered to say no to sin and yes to holy living. Is holiness important?

Hebrews 12:14

*Strive for peace with everyone, and for the **holiness without which no one will see the Lord**.*

The process of sanctification is very important...it affects whether we eventually see the Lord or not!

Romans 6:22

*But now that you have been set free from sin and have become slaves of God, the fruit you get leads to **sanctification and its end, eternal life**.*

Notice the powerful connection here between the process of sanctification and eternal life. I find it intriguing that the Apostle Paul used the word *sanctification* as the thing that leads to eternal life, not *justification*. It begs the question, "Well, what if someone rejects the process of sanctification?" It's implicit in the verse that eternal life would be in peril.

Sanctification is the process of being delivered from worldliness and then the subsequent partaking of God's nature of holiness.

2 Corinthians 6:17

Therefore go out from their midst, and be separate from them, says the Lord, and **touch no unclean thing; then I will welcome you.**

There is a God part and a man part to this process. God's part is the Holy Spirit empowering and transforming us. The believer's part is perseverance and faithfulness to Christ. In this sense, salvation is currently going on in believers.

Acts 2:47

And the Lord added to their number day by day those who **were being saved.**

1 Corinthians 15:2

And by which **you are being saved**, *if you hold fast to the word I preached to you—unless you believed in vain.*

Philippians 2:12

Therefore, my beloved, as you have always obeyed, so now, not only as in my presence but much more in my absence, **work out your own salvation with fear and trembling.**

1 Corinthians 1:18

The cross is folly to those who are perishing, but to us **who are being saved** *it is the power of God.*

You were saved, and you are being saved.

Future - Glorification

The future aspect of salvation is at the second coming of Christ, what we call glorification. This is when we receive new, glorified bodies, when *this perishable body puts on the imperishable, and this mortal body puts on immortality*, 1 Corinthians 15:53. It's when we begin to enjoy the final state of a newly recreated heaven and earth (Revelation 21:1,2). Therefore, in this sense, the completion of salvation is future.

Romans 5:9

*Since, therefore, we **have now been justified** by his blood, much more **shall we be saved** by him from the wrath of God.*

Romans 13:11

*Besides this you know the time, that the hour has come for you to wake from sleep. **For salvation is nearer to us now than when we first believed.***

Evidently salvation wasn't completed when we first believed!

Philippians 1:6

*And I am sure of this, that he who began a good work in you will **bring it to completion at the day of Jesus Christ.***

The work that began in us (salvation) is an ongoing work, finding it's completion on the day of final redemption at the second coming of Christ.

1 Peter 1:5

*Who by God's power are being guarded through faith **for a salvation ready to be revealed in the last time.***

Note that God's power guards us, but not automatically. It's "through faith," meaning, our continued believing, following and trusting Him.

Matthew 24:13

*But the one who endures to the end **will be saved**.*

1 Corinthians 5:5

*You are to deliver this man to Satan for the destruction of the flesh, so that his spirit **may be saved in the day of the Lord**.*

Wait, I though his spirit was saved the moment he accepted Christ!

Acts 15:11

*But we believe that **we will be saved** through the grace of the Lord Jesus, just as they will.*

Romans 5:9-10

*Since, therefore, we **have now been justified** by his blood, **much more shall we be saved** by him from the wrath of God. For if while **we were enemies** we were reconciled to God by the death of his Son, much more, now that **we are reconciled, shall we be saved by his life**.*

Here was see all three:
Past: have now been justified
Present: we are reconciled
Future: much more shall we be saved by his life

All three; past, present and future, have one basic condition: faith coupled with continued faithfulness. As we've seen, the salvation journey can be interrupted when a believer chooses one of four things:

1. Chooses to reject and no longer believe in Christ.
2. Chooses to backslide into a continued lifestyle of sin.
3. Chooses complacency and lukewarmness over being hot.
4. Chooses to embrace heresy.

Salvation involves more than just saying a prayer at an altar call. It starts there but doesn't end there.

Chapter 10

Assurance of Salvation

The purpose of this book is to promote serious reflection on what it means to be a disciple and follower of Christ, along with an accurate biblical assessment of the requirements to attain eternal life. In doing so it's inevitable that some people will become unnecessarily anxious or even fearful. Healthy fear is not a bad thing.

Proverbs 3:7

*Be not wise in your own eyes; **fear the Lord**, and turn away from evil.*

At the same time, we don't have to be fearful and can feel secure in our salvation and eternal life if we understand and meet the conditions. Salvation is conditional, and seeing the process of salvation to its completion, glorification, is conditional as well. We have two choices when it comes to assurance for salvation after a person has accepted Christ:

1. Unconditional Eternal Security.

Once you have accepted Christ, there are no more conditions to experiencing eternal life. The one and only condition has been met...accepting Christ and inviting Him into your life. From that point on, your security is unconditional. Even if you never truly follow Christ from that point on, even if you live a lifestyle of sin until the day you die, you'll still going to heaven and experiencing eternal life.

2. Conditional Eternal Security.

Once you accept Christ, you are saved and have eternal life. But this salvation is conditional upon continuing to stay faithful to Christ. This doesn't mean there won't be times you sin, for we all sin. But it does mean that your life, as a whole, is not marked by a practice or lifestyle of sin or lukewarmness. For the most part, your life expresses faithfulness to Christ through continued love, worship and service to Him, along with works of obedience that are a result of faith and empowered by the Spirit.

I advocate for the second option, **conditional eternal security**, because I see this as the more biblical position. I have already, I believe, adequately shown from Scripture that it is possible for a saved or born-again person to forfeit their salvation. This could happen through four possible ways:

1. Rejection of Christ.
2. The practice of sin.
3. Lukewarmness.
4. False doctrine or heresy.

Revelation 3:5

> **All who are victorious** will be clothed in white. **I will never erase their names** from the Book of Life, but I will announce before my Father and his angels that they are mine. (NLT)

"All who are victorious" is best interpreted as staying faithful to Christ to the very end. It doesn't mean they were perfect, it doesn't mean they were sinless and didn't have periods of time when they struggled. It means, when we look at their life as a whole, they endured and stayed faithful to following Christ. We would interpret "all who are victorious" in harmony with Matthew 24:13, "But the one who endures to the end will be saved." This is confirmed in Revelation 2:7

Revelation 2:7

> **To the one who conquers** I will grant to eat of the tree of life, which is in the paradise of God.

What's implicit here is that if one doesn't conquer, they will not be granted the right to eat of the tree of life. Additionally, how does one conquer?

1 John 5:4

This is the victory *that has overcome the world—**our faith.***

We overcome through continued faith in Christ. We're saved by faith and maintained by faith. 'Continuing' is the key.

John 8:31

*So Jesus was saying to those Jews who had believed Him, "If you **continue** in My word, then you are truly disciples of Mine. (NASB)*

This gospel was given for a purpose—for just believing, or is there something else?

Romans 16:26

*To bring about **the obedience of faith.***

It wasn't given just to believe it, it was given to obey it.

The converse is true as well. Those who aren't victorious by staying faithful to Christ will have their names erased from the Book of Life. Jesus would never have said "I will never erase their names from the Book of Life" (Revelation 3:5) unless it was possible.

A big part of the problem is that most people see a difference between a Christian and a disciple. If I gave a group of people a test, and had them write down the difference between a *Christian* and a *disciple*, almost all of them would say a Christian is someone who believes in Jesus Christ, but a disciple is someone who is *really into it*, someone who reads the bible a lot, prays and goes to church regularly. It's like a disciple is a Christian on steroids. But in Scripture there is no such differentiation. The term "Christian" is used three times in Scripture, and every time the term is used by or is connected to outsiders in how they viewed or described Christ-followers (Acts 11:26, Acts 26:28, 1 Peter 4:16). The term "disciple" is the term Scripture uses for followers of Christ. Why is this important? Because of the ramifications of what Jesus said in Luke 14.

Luke 14:26-27,33

95

> *If anyone comes to me and does not hate his own father and mother and wife and children and brothers and sisters, yes, and even his own life, he **cannot be my disciple**. Whoever does not bear his own cross and come after me **cannot be my disciple**. So therefore, any one of you who does not renounce all that he has **cannot be my disciple**.*

If we read the passage using the word "Christian," it becomes a shocking truth.

> *If anyone comes to me and does not hate his own father and mother and wife and children and brothers and sisters, yes, and even his own life, he **cannot be a Christian**. Whoever does not bear his own cross and come after me **cannot be a Christian**. So therefore, any one of you who does not renounce all that he has **cannot be a Christian**.*

What if we started defining a Christian in biblical terms instead of, "someone who accepted Christ and said the sinner's prayer a while back"?

If it's possible for someone to forfeit salvation, then our assurance of salvation must be something other than the fact that we accepted Christ X number of years ago. As I show in this this book, salvation is a process that starts the moment we accept Christ, but continues into the present and onward into the future. Final salvation is *realized* when we die and enter Paradise. Our present assurance of being saved must be derived another way. I'll show in Chapters 13, 14 and 15 a way to test ourselves to see if we are "in the faith." These chapters reference 1 John which gives us a way to find out if we're saved and have eternal life.

1 John 5:13

> **I write these things** to you who believe in the name of the Son of God, **that you may know that you have eternal life.**

Can we know we have eternal life? Yes we can know, and that's why the Apostle John wrote his letter we know as 1 John. In that letter he gives a criteria for how we can know. More on that later. The important principle to understand now is that eternal life is conditional NOT just because one said the *sinner's prayer* X number of years, but by other ways.

THE 'IFS'

The most frequent word denoting something being conditional is by the use of the word "if." As a young boy, when my father said, "You can go play with your friends *if* you get your chores done first," I knew there was a condition attached that I must comply with. We know promises are conditional by the use of the word "if." And so it is with Scripture.

1 John 2:24-25

If what you heard from the beginning abides in you, then you too will abide in the Son and in the Father. And this is the promise that he made to us—eternal life.

What if what we've heard from the beginning DOESN'T continue to abide in us? Would we still have eternal life? If we did, the verse would be meaningless because the apparent condition is not really a true condition at all.

1 Corinthians 15:2

(The gospel) by which you are being saved if you hold fast to the word I preached to you—unless you believed in vain.

It begs the question...and what if we don't continue to hold fast?

John 8:31

If you abide in my word, you are truly my disciples.

And what if you don't abide in His word, are you still a Christian?

Hebrews 3:6

Christ is faithful over God's house as a son. And we are his house, *if* *indeed we hold fast our confidence and our boasting in our hope.*

What if we don't hold fast our confidence and hope?

1 John 2:3

And by this we know that we have come to know him, *if* *we keep his commandments.*

If we don't keep His commandments, we don't know Him, even if we claim that we do.

Hebrews 3:14

For we have come to share in Christ, *if* *indeed we hold our original confidence firm to the end.*

What if we don't hold our original faith firm to the end?

Colossians 1:21-23

And you, who once were alienated and hostile in mind, doing evil deeds, he has now reconciled in his body of flesh by his death, in order to present you holy and blameless and above reproach before him, *if* *indeed you continue in the faith, stable and steadfast, not shifting from the hope of the gospel that you heard.*

What if we don't continue in faith, stable and steadfast, not shifting away from the hope of the gospel?

Being presented before God at judgment holy, blameless and above reproach is conditional on steadfastly continuing in the faith and not shifting away from it. If everyone who accepted Christ was automatically presented before God holy, blameless and above reproach at judgment because they said the sinner's prayer at some point of time in the past, these verses would be meaningless. But the Apostle Paul clearly connects our assurance to continuing to stay faithful to the Lord. Therefore, assurance of salvation now and on the day of judgment is connected to faithfulness to continue to love and serve the Lord, through Christ.

Philippians 2:14-16

Do all things without grumbling or disputing, that you may be **blameless** *and innocent, children of God without blemish in the midst of a crooked and twisted generation, among whom you shine as lights in the world,* **holding fast to the word of life**, *so that in the day of Christ I may be proud that I did not run in vain or labor in vain.*

Paul said the same thing here. He talked about being blameless (same word as Colossians), without blemish (Colossians said *without reproach*), in the day of Christ, which could be the second coming of Christ and/or the day of judgment. But notice the condition attached here..."holding fast to the word of life." Then we see the words "so that," which indicates what follows is the result of what preceded it. Holding fast to the word of life means faithfulness, resulting in being presented before Christ blameless and without reproach. Therefore assurance is conditional on staying faithful to Jesus Christ. Faith, continued faith, a faith with corresponding works, is the condition to being saved, and faith (faithfulness) is the condition to staying saved.

2 Peter 1:10

For (**if**) *you practice these qualities you will never fall.*

Not drifting away from Christ or falling is connected to staying faithful to practice one's faith.

"If" in the scriptures above shows these promises are conditional. Sharing in Christ is conditional upon staying faithful and holding onto our original confidence (faith), FIRM TO THE END.

1 Peter 1:3-5

To an inheritance that is imperishable, undefiled, and unfading, kept in heaven for you, who by God's power are being guarded **through faith** *for a salvation ready to be revealed in the last time.*

Experiencing salvation and our heavenly inheritance comes as a result of God's power to keep and guard us, which is secured *through faith.* We are being guarded through continued faith for this salvation.

Hebrews 10:38-39

> ***My righteous one shall live by faith,*** *and **if** he shrinks back, my soul has no pleasure in him. But we are not of those who shrink back and are destroyed, but of those who have faith and preserve their souls.*

Living in continued faith preserves the soul, but shrinking back from an active faith results in destruction. Therefore, our assurance of salvation is connected to not shrinking back, but continuing in faith, or by continued living by faith (*my righteous one shall LIVE by faith*).

To put it succinctly, our assurance in salvation is staying faithful to Christ. Assurance is based upon staying faithful to the Bridegroom. The test of genuineness of a man's faith is not determined by his vows, but by his life.

There are other verses in Scripture where "if" is implied. For example:

John 15:4

> *Remain in me, and I will remain in you. (NLT)*

Jesus remaining in us is conditional upon us remaining in Him.

BUYING SALVATION

Did you know that you can buy salvation? It's true, Scripture says so. But it's not with the currency of money, it's with a different kind of currency.

Isaiah 55:1-2

> *Come, everyone who thirsts, come to the waters; and he who has no money, come, **buy** and eat! Come, **buy** wine and milk without money and without price. Why do you spend your money for that which is not bread, and your labor for that which does not satisfy?*

The exiles in Babylon were told to buy spiritual refreshment from the Lord, not with money, but with faith.

Matthew 25:8-10

*And the foolish said to the wise, 'Give us some of your oil, for our lamps are going out.' But the wise answered, saying, 'Since there will not be enough for us and for you, go rather to the dealers and **buy** for yourselves.' And while they were going to **buy**, the bridegroom came, and those who were ready went in with him to the marriage feast, and the door was shut.*

The five foolish virgins were lacking what it took (oil) to gain entrance to the wedding feast when the bridegroom came for them. They were told to go buy oil for themselves so they could be part of the wedding party. This parable is about being ready spiritually for the second coming of Christ. Buying oil represents staying spiritually prepared through continued faith and spiritual watchfulness, looking for the Bridegroom. We buy oil necessary for entrance to the wedding feast with the bridegroom through faithfulness.

Revelation 3:15-19

*I know your works: you are neither cold nor hot. Would that you were either cold or hot! So, because you are lukewarm, and neither hot nor cold, I will spit you out of my mouth. For you say, I am rich, I have prospered, and I need nothing, not realizing that you are wretched, pitiable, poor, blind, and naked. I **counsel you to buy from me gold refined by fire**, so that you may be rich, and white garments so that you may clothe yourself and the shame of your nakedness may not be seen, and salve to anoint your eyes, so that you may see. Those whom I love, I reprove and discipline, so be zealous and repent.*

The people mentioned here didn't realize how wretched, naked and lacking they were. Jesus' instructions to them, "Buy from Me gold refined by fire." This would result in their salvation, now being clothed with righteousness. We buy this, not with money, but with faith and staying faithful to follow Jesus Christ. Assurance is based on continued faith and faithfulness to Christ, not a prayer said X number of years ago at an altar call.

Chapter 11

Recognize Them by Their Fruit

The problem of false and forfeited conversions is pervasive. Jesus taught (Matthew 7:21-23) that *many* on the day of judgment will call Him "Lord," but Jesus will say to them that He never knew them because their behavior wasn't in harmony with their profession of faith.

Jesus also taught that we'll be able to recognize the people who profess Him but deny Him by their behavior.

Matthew 7:15-20

15 *Beware of false prophets, who come to you in sheep's clothing but inwardly are ravenous wolves.*

16 ***You will recognize them by their fruits.*** *Are grapes gathered from thornbushes, or figs from thistles?*

17 *So, every healthy tree bears good fruit, but the diseased tree bears bad fruit.*

18 *A healthy tree cannot bear bad fruit, nor can a diseased tree bear good fruit.*

19 *Every tree that does not bear good fruit is cut down and thrown into the fire.*

20 ***Thus you will recognize them by their fruits.***

Although this talks about "false prophets" and how to recognize them, by extension and application, the passage also applies to false disciples. Why would Jesus say "you will recognize them" if He didn't want us to recognize them?

"You will recognize them" gives us permission, NOT to give final condemnation and judgment, but to simply note and discern who is "talking the talk" but not "walking the walk." The accusation at this point is, "Who appointed you to be a fruit inspector?" In one sense, Jesus did. In another sense, to be clear, we're not called to go around with the intention of analyzing professing believers' fruit. At the same time, when the situation arises naturally, Jesus gave us a way to tell if someone is *walking the walk* and not just *talking the talk*.

"Fruit" here is a metaphor for behavior, conduct, deeds or works. The relationship that Jesus taught is simple and clear:

Bad fruit = bad tree
Good fruit = good tree

We can also see this relationship from John 15.

John 15:1-6

1   *I am the true vine, and my Father is the vinedresser.*

2   *Every branch in me that does not bear **fruit** he takes away, and every branch that does bear **fruit** he prunes, that it may bear more **fruit**.*

3   *Already you are clean because of the word that I have spoken to you.*

4   *Abide in me, and I in you. As the branch cannot bear **fruit** by itself, unless it abides in the vine, neither can you, unless you abide in me.*

5   *I am the vine; you are the branches. Whoever abides in me and I in him, he it is that bears much **fruit**, for apart from me you can do nothing.*

6   *If anyone does not abide in me he is thrown away like a branch and withers; and the branches are gathered, thrown into the fire, and burned.*

Jesus taught that fruit-bearing is critically important, so much so that if a branch wasn't bearing fruit, it was cut off and thrown into the fire. However, if a branch is vitally connected to the vine, it will produce fruit. A lack of fruit-bearing indicates that there is something wrong in that connection, and I can assure you it doesn't have anything to do with the vine. It's a branch problem.

If a person's life doesn't possess conduct consistent with *repent, believe, receive, follow*—we have every right to be skeptical about the true status of their salvation.

Matthew 3:8

Prove by the way you live *that you have repented of your sins and turned to God. (NLT)*

Acts 26:20

I preached that they should repent and turn to God and **demonstrate their repentance by their deeds.** *(NIV)*

Jesus said, "You'll recognize them by their fruits." Again, we don't have the authority to condemn or issue final judgment upon them, that comes when they die (Hebrews 9:27 – "It is appointed for man to die once, and after that comes judgment"). Final judgment belongs to God alone. Yet Jesus clearly taught that we can and should discern and recognize whether it's a good or bad tree based on their conduct. This, of course, involves making a judgment of some kind...good fruit or bad fruit? The word "judge" simply means to weigh evidence and form an opinion. "You'll recognize them by their fruits" certainly would involve that.

WHAT ABOUT "JUDGE NOT?"

It's at this point inevitably someone will say, "Hey, wait a minute, Jesus said 'Judge not lest you be judged!'" You're correct, Jesus did say that. In fact, He said that at the beginning of this very same chapter, Matthew 7, the chapter about recognizing people by their fruit.

Matthew 7:1

Judge not, that you be not judged.

Because this verse is so often misinterpreted and misapplied, I'm going to take time to delve into it.

Usually someone will say something like, "We're all sinners, who am I to judge?" or "Yes, he cheated on his wife, but who am I to judge? After all, Jesus said, 'Judge not lest you be judged.'" Matthew 7:1 is taken to mean that you mustn't judge or speak up about anything.

You mean, if you were living in the year 1800 during the time of the ruthless slave traders shipping blacks from Africa to America, you'd keep quiet over their sinful behavior because after all Jesus said, "Judge not lest you be judged?" That's not how William Wilberforce thought. He was an English politician, who, after becoming a Christian in 1785, started the English abolition movement to stop the slave trade. Thank God William Wilberforce judged wicked behavior and spoke up. His story is told in the wonderful 2006 movie "Amazing Grace."

Matthew 7:1 is the go-to verse used to shut down all discussion when someone expresses an unfavorable opinion on abortion, homosexuality, gay marriage, polyamory or other moral issues. Even Pope Francis, in chatting with reporters on a plane in July 2013, used this popular "judge not" mantra.

Replied when asked about the Vatican's alleged "gay lobby" that while a lobby might be an issue, he doesn't have any problem with the inclination to homosexuality itself: "Who am I to judge them if they're seeking the Lord in good faith?" he said.[11]

What's implied is that no one can ever say something is morally wrong or that a certain behavior is sinful. All of this is based on a misinterpretation of Matthew 7:1 (*Judge not, that you be not judged*).

Now at first glance, if you take this verse all by itself without keeping the verse in context with the passage it sits in, it seems like an unconditional declaration to never judge anyone. But we must interpret this verse (and all verses for that matter) in context with the passage surrounding it as well as with the rest of Scripture. The word "context" comes from a compound Latin word, *con* (together) and *textus* (to weave). So, *context* means

---

[11]   National Catholic Reporter – Pope on Homosexuals: Who am I to judge? - https://www.ncronline.org/blogs/ncr-today/pope-homo-sexuals-who-am-i-judge

understanding that a verse is woven together into the fabric of the whole passage that it's sitting in. Taking things out of context causes misinterpretation, both in Scripture and in life in general.

For example, someone on a sweltering 115-degree sunny day might say, "It's so hot, I'm telling you, I'd kill for an air conditioner." At this point, someone could call 911 and tell them, "I heard him say he was going to kill someone, come quick!" But once examining the context in which it was said, the problem would easily be resolved.

We must also interpret a verse in harmony with the rest of Scripture. If that supposed truth doesn't square with the rest of Scripture, then we should correctly assume it's a wrong interpretation. So let's look at the passage to see its context.

If we take verse 1 in context with verses 2 through 5, we see that Jesus is teaching that it's wrong to judge someone else when we are guilty of the same things. "Judge not lest you be judge" is NOT a prohibition against judging, it's a prohibition against hypocrisy.

Matthew 7:1-5

1   *Judge not, that you be not judged.*

2   *For with the judgment you pronounce you will be judged, and with the measure you use it will be measured to you.*

3   *Why do you see the speck that is in your brother's eye, **but do not notice the log that is in your own eye?***

4   *Or how can you say to your brother, 'Let me take the speck out of your eye,' **when there is the log in your own eye?***

5   ***You hypocrite, first** take the log out of your own eye, and **then** you will see clearly to take the speck out of your brother's eye.*

In the context of the passage verse 1 sits in, we have two possibilities of interpretation:

1. We should never judge anyone else...ever!

2. We shouldn't be hypocrites by judging others while doing the same things.

The context makes it clear, Jesus was addressing the problem
of judging someone while doing the very same things! He's saying,
"If you can't hold to the same standard, then you have no business
applying that standard to other people." In other words,
hypocrisy, not judgment, was the issue Jesus was addressing!
Verse 5 starts out with the words, "You hypocrite!"

It couldn't mean that you can never make moral judgments
because look at the very next verse:

Matthew 7:6

*Do not give dogs what is holy, and do not throw your pearls
before pigs, lest they trample them underfoot and turn to attack
you.*

In order to obey this verse, wouldn't you have to make a
moral judgment on who's a dog or pig? This verse requires a
judgment to be made! Not only that, but in the very same chapter,
Matthew 7, look again at verses 15 to 20.

Matthew 7:15-20

15 **Beware of false prophets**, *who come to you in sheep's
clothing but inwardly are ravenous wolves.*

16 **You will recognize them** *by their fruits. Are grapes
gathered from thornbushes, or figs from thistles?*

17 *So, every healthy tree bears good fruit, but the diseased tree
bears bad fruit.*

18 *A healthy tree cannot bear bad fruit, nor can a diseased tree
bear good fruit.*

19 *Every tree that does not bear good fruit is cut down and
thrown into the fire.*

20 **Thus you will recognize them** *by their fruits.*

We're commanded to identify and beware of false prophets. That takes a judgment (weigh evidence and form an opinion). We're commanded to recognize people based on the fruit they are bearing, again, that involves making a judgment. Keep in mind, this is just a few verses down from "Judge not lest you be judged."

When Jesus said "Judge not lest you be judged" He was talking about not judging people in a hypocritical fashion. Is this interpretation (judging related to hypocrisy) in harmony with the rest of Scripture? Yes!

Romans 2:1-3

1   *Therefore you have no excuse, O man, every one of you who judges. For in passing judgment on another **you condemn yourself, because you, the judge, practice the very same things.***

2   *We know that the judgment of God rightly falls on those who practice such things.*

3   *Do you suppose, O man—you who judge those who practice such things **and yet do them yourself**—that you will escape the judgment of God?*

Romans 2 sheds light on the correct interpretation of Matthew 7:1! It's judging while being hypocritical...doing the same things!

Besides that, how can "Judge not lest you be judged" mean never making moral judgments about sin when we're commanded in Scripture to do that very thing?

Philippians 3:2

Look out for the dogs, look out for the evildoers.

This would require one to make a moral judgment on what is sin and what isn't—who's an evildoer and who isn't. What's even wilder is something Jesus said in John 7.

John 7:24

*Stop judging by mere appearances, but instead **judge correctly**. (NIV)*

So we are to judge, but we're to judge correctly. If we were not to judge at all, Jesus here would have contradicted what He said in Matthew 7:1.

In 1 Corinthians 5 Paul is rebuking the Christians in the city of Corinth for putting up (and even boasting about their tolerance) with someone living in sexual immorality. Listen to what Paul says:

1 Corinthians 5:1-2

It is actually reported that there is sexual immorality among you...and you are arrogant! Ought you not rather to mourn? Let him who has done this be removed from among you.

The Corinthians were actually boasting about their tolerance of sin instead of speaking up about it! This is exactly what is happening today!

1 Corinthians 5:6-7

Your boasting is not good. Do you not know that a little leaven leavens the whole lump? Cleanse out the old leaven that you may be a new lump, as you really are unleavened.

Instead of being vexed about sexual immorality in the church, they not only tolerated it but were proud of themselves for tolerating it! Isn't identifying sexual immorality within the church "judging?" Of course it is. So was Paul contradicting Jesus? Not at all. Jesus didn't mean that we can't judge, but that we don't judge while doing the same things, thereby being hypocritical.

We must keep Matthew 7:1 in harmony with the rest of Scripture because there is a time and place to judge.

1 Corinthians 5:3-5

3   *For though absent in body, I am present in spirit; and as if present, I have already **pronounced judgment** on the one who did such a thing.*

4   *When you are assembled in the name of the Lord Jesus and my spirit is present, with the power of our Lord Jesus,*

5 *you are to deliver this man to Satan for the destruction of the flesh, so that his spirit may be saved in the day of the Lord.*

How could Paul pronounce judgment when Jesus instructed us not to judge lest we be judged? Was the Apostle Paul out of order for judging believers' behavior? No!

1 Corinthians 5:11-13

11 *But now I am writing to you not to associate with anyone who bears the name of brother if he is guilty of sexual immorality or greed, or is an idolater, reviler, drunkard, or swindler—not even to eat with such a one.*

12 *For what have I to do with **judging** outsiders? **Is it not those inside the church whom you are to judge?***

13 *God **judges** those outside. "Purge the evil person from among you."*

The subject here is judging people within the church, those who profess Christ but who are living in sin. Some kind of judgment would be necessary in order to do this.

James 5:19-20

My brothers, if anyone among you wanders from the truth and someone brings him back, let him know that whoever brings back a sinner from his wandering will save his soul from death and will cover a multitude of sins.

In order to obey these verses, a judgment would need to be made whether someone was wandering from the truth and living in sin. This is not a contradiction to Matthew 7:1, "Judge not lest you be judged," which is talking about judging people hypocritically while doing the same things. It is NOT saying that we can never judge something or someone as far as sin or bad fruit.

And to be clear, there's a difference between making a legitimate moral judgment and being *judgmental*. We all make moral judgments (what is right and wrong) every day. That's healthy. Being *judgmental* is when someone is **excessively critical**, it's the tendency to **judge too harshly or quickly**. "You're being judgmental!" "No, I'm making a simple moral judgment based on God's Word as a standard of right and wrong." So there's a difference between making moral judgments and being judgmental!

Additionally, there's a difference between making moral judgments of what is right and wrong and setting oneself up as the final judge who pronounces a sentence. No one can do that but God alone.

James 4:12

> There is only one lawgiver and judge, he who is able to save and to destroy.

We don't have the power or authority to pronounce a sentence or punishment on people. That is God alone, but we do have the right and responsibility to make moral judgments on right and wrong. Someone in the jury box is making a moral judgment on behavior, but they are not the judge who pronounces a sentence and punishment. So Matthew 7:1, "Judge not lest you be judged," is misinterpreted almost 100% of the time, but it's clear from Scripture that it means "don't judge hypocritically while doing the same things, do not judge unfairly."

Matthew 7:15-20 teaches that we will recognize true followers of Jesus Christ by their fruit. Good fruit means a good tree, bad fruit means a bad tree. Keep in mind the very next verses that follow in Matthew 7 are verses we've read before, verses 21-23 which continue with the theme of the possibility of people professing to know Christ but who aren't saved:

Matthew 7:21-23

> 21 Not everyone who says to me, "Lord, Lord," will enter the kingdom of heaven, but the one who **does the will of my Father** who is in heaven.

> 22 On that day many will say to me, "Lord, Lord, did we not prophesy in your name, and cast out demons in your name, and do many mighty works in your name?"

23   *And then will I declare to them, "**I never knew you**; depart from me, you **workers of lawlessness.**"*

The subject here is people who think they're saved but really aren't. If someone has biblical faith and is truly, genuinely born again, the result will be a changed life. If may not be immediately, but sooner or later it must result in a changed life or else...bad fruit/bad tree.

2 Corinthians 5:17

Therefore, if anyone is in Christ, he is a new creation. The old has passed away; behold, the new has come.

If the past prayer or decision didn't produce a new, changed life eventually, then we have every right to be skeptical whether the person's born-again experience embraced the elements mentioned earlier: *repent, believe, receive* and *follow.*

Matthew 7 gave a test for discerning whether others seem to be born again by observing their behavior and conduct over the long run. If God didn't want us to be able to observe and discern this, why did He say for us to do exactly that?

I believe God wants us to observe and discern bad fruit/bad tree versus good fruit/good tree for two main reasons:

1. As a warning for us to keep mindful and aware of our own walk with God, ensuring that we enter through the narrow gate and keep to the narrow road.

1 Corinthians 10:12

*Therefore let anyone who thinks that he stands **take heed lest he fall.***

Galatians 6:1

*Brothers, if anyone is caught in any transgression, you who are spiritual should restore him in a spirit of gentleness. **Keep watch on yourself, lest you too be tempted.***

Being aware that we could slip ourselves helps to keep our guard up. But there's another reason Jesus commanded us to discern good & bad trees.

2.   To exhort and warn those caught in the bad fruit/bad tree condition to move past an empty profession of faith to the reality of the full born-again experience. Their eternity depends on this.

Ezekiel 3:19

If you do warn the wicked person and they do not turn from their wickedness or from their evil ways, they will die for their sin; but you will have saved yourself.

Jude 1:23

Save others by snatching them out of the fire.

God expects us to warn people of the consequences of their sin and invite them to repent and turn to Christ. We are remiss if we don't.

TAKING INVENTORY OF OUR OWN FRUIT

Jesus said, "You'll recognize them by their fruit." The flip side of the same coin is people recognizing us by *our* fruit. We need to make sure it's evident *we're* growing in faith.

1 Timothy 4:15

*Be diligent in these matters; give yourself wholly to them, **so that everyone may see your progress.** (NIV)*

We are to recognize others by *their* fruit, but they are to recognize us by *our* fruit. And we are told to be diligent in fruit-bearing so that it's obvious to all. It's two sides of the same coin. When people look at your life, do they see spiritual growth, a changed life, a life submitted to the Lordship of Jesus Christ? Answering 'no' indicates that a change is needed. According to that verse and its preceding verses, spiritual progress is the direct result of "giving yourself wholly to" God and the goal of spiritual growth. "Giving yourself wholly to" the things of God and the Lordship of Jesus Christ therefore, is the place of our focus.

But how do we know if we're growing spiritually and staying faithful to Christ?

Chapter 12

Test Yourselves

Whereas Matthew 7:21-23 (*I never knew you; depart from me, you workers of lawlessness*) and Titus 1:16 (*they profess to know God, but they deny him by their works*) talk about *others*, what about *us*? Should we assess our own lives regarding these things, and if so, how do we do that? The answer to both questions is "yes." Yes we should assess our own lives (1 Timothy 4:15 – *so that all may see your progress*), and yes there IS a way to do that.

2 Corinthians 13:5

> **Examine yourselves**, *to see whether you are in the faith.* **Test yourselves.** *Or do you not realize this about yourselves, that Jesus Christ is in you?—***unless indeed you fail to meet the test!**

This isn't a suggestion...it's a command. We are commanded to examine and test ourselves to discern whether Jesus Christ is really in us and that we are truly saved. And the Apostle Paul here is talking to church people, he's addressing people who believe they're saved but may not be! The intent here is not to navel-gaze until we're ridden with anxiety or guilt. The intent is to look at our lives to ensure we're living out our profession of faith—that we're living lives of devotion, commitment, obedience, service and holiness before God. We're to examine ourselves to see if there's fruit consistent with true, biblical faith.

2 Peter 1:10

> *Therefore, brothers,* **be all the more diligent to confirm your calling and election,** *for if you practice these qualities you will never fall.*

Question: Why would you need to confirm, not just *confirm*, but be **diligent** *to confirm* something you did twenty years ago when you repeated "the sinners' prayer" at an altar call and got "saved?" Answer: Because if there is no fruit or works (mentioned in the preceding verses) that correspond to that act, it didn't result in a genuine born-again experience, or...one has drifted into rejection of Christ or lukewarmness.

The phrase "your calling" refers to the call or invitation extended to us by God to receive His Son, Jesus Christ (2 Peter 1:3 - *him who **called** us to his own glory and excellence*). The word *election* refers to God's act of *electing* or *choosing* for salvation all those He knew would respond to His invitation. Election is based on God's "foreknowledge."

Romans 8:29

*For **those whom he foreknew** he also predestined to be conformed to the image of his Son.*

1 Peter 1:1,2

*Peter, an apostle of Jesus Christ, to those who are **elect** exiles of the Dispersion in Pontus, Galatia, Cappadocia, Asia, and Bithynia, **according to the foreknowledge of God the Father**, in the sanctification of the Spirit, for obedience to Jesus Christ and for sprinkling with his blood*

God knew beforehand who would accept Him and who wouldn't. To those who responded to His call, He choose them to be part of *the elect* (Titus 1:1), those chosen to receive eternal life. The invitation or call has gone out to everyone, but only a few respond (Matthew 22:14 - *many are called, but few are chosen*). To put it another way:

God votes for you.
Satan votes for you.
You cast the deciding vote.

Example: I'm the seventh-grade boys' baseball coach. I extend an invitation to all the seventh-grade boys to be part of the team, but only twelve boys accept the invitation. It's that group who responded to my call that I choose to take on a bus trip to see a major-league baseball game. I chose that group because they are the ones who responded to my invitation. The call went out to many, but only a few were chosen to go on the trip...those who responded. Many are called, few are chosen. (The analogy isn't perfect however because in God's case, He knew in advance who would respond to the invitation.) Back to our verse:

2 Peter 1:10

*Therefore, brothers, **be all the more diligent to confirm your calling and election,** for if you practice these qualities you will never fall.*

The phrase "your calling and election" therefore, refers to those saved—those who have eternal life. The very next verse confirms this.

2 Peter 1:11

*For **in this way** there will be richly provided for you an **entrance into the eternal kingdom** of our Lord and Savior Jesus Christ*

Notice the words, "in this way." Question: In what way? Answer: By being diligent to confirm your entrance into the eternal kingdom by being saved... part of the *elect*, those who've said 'yes' to God's invitation. *Be all the more diligent to confirm your calling and election.* OK, but how do we confirm we're part of this group—those called and elected? In the same chapter, go back a few verses, to verse 8.

2 Peter 1:8

*For **if these qualities are yours and are increasing,** they keep you from being ineffective or **unfruitful** in the knowledge of our Lord Jesus Christ.*

If these qualities are in you, it proves you have fruit. The verse says that not having these qualities is *unfruitful*. We confirm God's calling and election in our lives by examining them to see if we're experiencing these qualities and that these qualities are increasing. What qualities? Go back three verses prior.

2 Peter 1:5-7

*For this very reason, make every effort to **add to your faith** goodness; and to goodness, knowledge; and to knowledge, self-control; and to self-control, perseverance; and to perseverance, godliness; and to godliness, mutual affection; and to mutual affection, love. (NIV)*

Add to your faith these character fruits! The Apostle Peter is telling them that they have faith in Christ, which is great, but now to their faith they need to add these qualities or fruit to confirm that it's a genuine faith. Faith is the root, these qualities and good works are the fruit.

If we take 2 Peter 1:5-11 as a whole, we arrive at this truth:

> Now that you have faith, confirm it's a genuine faith by making sure you demonstrate fruit.

2 Corinthians 13:5 and 2 Peter 1:10 instruct us to examine our lives to confirm if we are in the faith and have entrance into God's eternal kingdom.

Again, this is not meant to produce anxiety, but simply as an exhortation to diligently look at our lives to ensure we're living with Jesus as Lord, which is the central message of this book.

Is there a way to tell if we're saved? Is there some kind of checklist we can use in examining ourselves to see if we're "in the faith?" The answer is 'yes.' The Apostle John gives us such a checklist, and we'll look at that in our next three chapters.

Chapter 13

Evidence for Faith – Part 1

The last few chapters dealt with the fact from scripture that there are false conversions, and that we will recognize them by their fruit. We've seen that just "professing" that Jesus is Lord is no indicator one is saved. We saw this from Matthew 7:21-23. It begs the question, "Well, how do we know we're saved? How can we have assurance that we have eternal life? Is there way to know?" The Apostle John helps us out with that.

1 John 5:13

> **I write these things** to you who believe in the name of the Son of God, **that you may know that you have eternal life**.

One reason the letter of 1 John was written was so we could know whether we have eternal life or not. At the end of the letter, after describing what a life submitted to the Lordship of Jesus Christ looks like, the Apostle John says (my paraphrase), "I wrote **these things** so that you can test and examine your lives so that you can know whether or not you have eternal life. If these things are evident in your life, you can know that you have eternal life."

So what are the "these things" that the Apostle John talked about? What is the criteria for helping us to know whether we have eternal life or not? I'll mention ten things from 1 John. The list is not exhaustive, but it's a good start.

EVIDENCE OF ETERNAL LIFE

1. **Fellowship with the Father, Son and other believers.**

1 John 1:3

*So that you too may have **fellowship with us**; and indeed **our fellowship is with the Father and with his Son Jesus Christ.***

The typical mistake here is to think fellowship is superficial talk about sports or fashion at a bean supper. Actually, bean suppers are a good way to destroy fellowship, but that's another story. Scripturally, "fellowship" is a powerful Greek word, **koinōnia**. Here the word means *intimate, close-knit community*. And who is our fellowship with?

WITH JESUS CHRIST

We are called to have this intimate, close-knit community with God through Jesus Christ.

1 Corinthians 1:9

*God is faithful, by whom you were called into the **fellowship** of his Son, Jesus Christ our Lord.*

It's the same Greek word used here as 1 John 1:3, *fellowship*. We're to have intimate, close-knit fellowship with God through Jesus Christ. With true believers, the evidence of this would be a lifestyle expressing that Jesus Christ is first-place in their lives above all else, namely: worship, prayer, Bible study, meditation upon God and His Word, obedience, walking in love, progress toward holiness and steady steps toward spiritual growth. If one doesn't engage with Christ through these activities, it is doubtful that God is preeminent in their lives. Chapter 22 of this book covers more ways to tell if we're in a true relationship with God through Christ.

Here in our first point we're really stating that Jesus Christ has preeminence in one's life. If someone asked you, "What's the most important thing in your life?" how would you respond? Your spouse? Your children? Career? Your friends? Helping and serving others? Your church? Any answer short of your relationship with God through Jesus Christ would be problematic. First things must be first.

Matthew 6:33

But seek first the kingdom of God and his righteousness, and all these things will be added to you.

Colossians 1:18

*And he (Jesus Christ) is the head of the body, the church. He is the beginning, the firstborn from the dead, **that in everything he might be preeminent.***

There are no close seconds. Fellowship, an intimate, close-knit relationship with God through His Son Jesus Christ is of primary importance to genuine Christ-followers. Everything else must pale in comparison. Jesus clearly taught this. At the end of Luke 14, it says that Jesus turned around and saw multitudes of people following Him. And turning to them He said something shocking.

Luke 14:25-27

Now great crowds accompanied him, and he turned and said to them, "If anyone comes to me and does not hate his own father and mother and wife and children and brothers and sisters, yes, and even his own life, he cannot be my disciple. Whoever does not bear his own cross and come after me cannot be my disciple.

If Tom Peers would have written this, it would read this way: "Now great crowds accompanied him, and he turned and said to them, 'God loves you and has a wonderful plan for your life. He wants to answer all your prayers and bless you with health, prosperity, a great complexion and a smoking-hot spouse.'" But, thank God, that's not what Jesus said.

Someone reading these verses may think, "To be Jesus' disciple I have to hate my spouse? Awesome, I'm all in!" But hold on, here "hate" should be interpreted to mean "love less in comparison to." Compared to the magnitude of love we have for Jesus, love for our family should almost seem like hate. This is what we mean by "fellowship with God." Jesus is first, He has preeminence "in everything."

It's obvious here in Luke 14 that Jesus was throwing out a filter to thin out the crowds. He did this to clearly communicate what it means to be His disciple...a follower, not just a fan. He wants everyone to follow Him, but on the correct terms—full devotion. That's why later in the passage it talks about counting the cost.

WITH OTHER BELIEVERS

We're also to have this intimate, close-knit community with other believers, the Body of Christ, which is the church.

1 John 1:3

*That which we have seen and heard we proclaim also to you, **so that you too may have fellowship with us**; and indeed our fellowship is with the Father and with his Son Jesus Christ.*

Acts 2:42

*And they devoted themselves to the apostles' teaching and the **fellowship**, to the breaking of bread and the prayers.*

This is the same Greek word as in 1 John 1:3, *fellowship*. The evidence of this in a believer's life would be regular *participation* (another definition of the Greek word *koinonia*) in a local church with other Christians. This speaks of regular attendance.

Hebrews 10:24-25

*And let us consider how to stir up one another to love and good works, **not neglecting to meet together, as is the habit of some**, but encouraging one another, and all the more as you see the Day drawing near.*

If a person does not possess the habit of regularly meeting with other Christians for worship, teaching, prayer, the Lord's supper and fellowship, it would be one indicator that they profess Christ, but don't exhibit the fruit of a genuine faith in Him.

2. **We walk in the light (holiness) and choose not walk in darkness (sin).**

1 John 1:5-6

*God is light, and in him is no darkness at all. If we say we have fellowship with him while **we walk in darkness**, we lie and do not practice the truth.*

"Walk in darkness" means a couple different things: 1) disconnected from Jesus Christ, the true light (John 8:12), and 2) living in sin. Walking in the light includes the converse: 1) A life vitally connected and committed to God through Christ, and 2) walking in holiness.

Regarding holiness and sin, walking in the light is a coin with two sides—saying yes to holiness and no to sin. If we say we're connected to the Light (God) but walking in darkness (sin), we're lying. Those truly born again will experience transformation.

1 John 2:29

*If you know that he is righteous, you may be sure that everyone who **practices** righteousness has been born of him.*

How do we know we're born again? We practice righteousness. "Practice" speaks of continuing behavior, not a one-time decision.

1 John 5:18

*We know that everyone who has been born of God does not **keep on sinning**.*

1 John 3:6

*No one who abides in him **keeps on sinning**; no one who **keeps on sinning** has either seen him or known him.*

Continuing a lifestyle of sin denotes someone not abiding in Christ. This means that a true believer eliminates behavior that is displeasing to God.

1 John 3:3

*And everyone who thus hopes in him **purifies himself** as he is pure.*

The issue here is NOT that we sin. We all sin. The issue is PRACTICING sin, in other words, intentional, willful sin which continues over the course of one's life without genuine repentance, which would contradict fruit-bearing consistent with someone truly born again.

3. We are sensitive to our sin and God's conviction of it. We are quick to confess and repent.

1 John 1:9

If we confess our sins, he is faithful and just to forgive us our sins and to cleanse us from all unrighteousness.

Psalm 32:5

I acknowledged my sin to you, and I did not cover my iniquity; I said, "I will confess my transgressions to the LORD," and you forgave the iniquity of my sin.

True disciples of Jesus Christ will sense conviction from the Holy Spirit when they sin. When they do, they are quick to confess their sin before God and receive forgiveness.

There is a growing group of Christians that teach that you really don't have to do that. "Hyper-grace" teachers claim that this verse, 1 John 1:9, is not written to or about Christians. They say that because of the completed work of Christ on the cross, we have already been forgiven for all of our sins: past, present and future. They say 1 John 1:9 is written to and about those in the church who are lost and regards their initial repentance connected to the born-again experience (repent and believe). In his book, *Hyper-Grace*, Dr. Michael L. Brown talks about this.

"Since hyper-grace teachers believe that the moment we are saved, God pronounces all our sins forgiven—meaning, past, present, and future sins—they also believe that there is no need . for us to confess our sins to God as believers or to ask for forgiveness. As expressed by Paul Ellis, 'Forgiveness seems to be

a blind spot for many people. We just can't get it into our heads
that God has forgiven us completely and for all time."[12]

Hyper-grace teachers say that when we sin as Christians, we don't have to act on 1 John 1:9 and confess our sins. No...all we must do is a quick acknowledgement that we blew it and move on...a quick "oopsy." That interpretation of 1 John 1:9 is significantly flawed. The Apostle John consistently uses the pronoun "we," "our" and "us" throughout his epistle, always referring to believers. Just one verse earlier, verse 8, it says, "If **we** say **we** have no sin, **we** deceive ourselves, and the truth is not in **us**." That's written to believers. To all of a sudden one verse later say that the "we" of 1 John 1:9 (*if we confess our sins*) means unbelievers, defies logic. When the Apostle John talks about those outside of the faith, he uses the pronouns *they* or *them*. Notice the contradistinction between you/us/we and they.

1 John 2:18-20

18 *Children, it is the last hour, and as <u>you</u> have heard*
   that antichrist is coming, so now many antichrists have
   come. Therefore <u>we</u> know that it is the last hour.

19 ***They** went out from <u>us</u>, but **they** were not of <u>us</u>; for if **they***
   *had been of <u>us</u>, **they** would have continued with <u>us</u>. But **they***
   *went out, that it might become plain that **they** all are not of*
   <u>us</u>.

20 *But <u>you</u> have been anointed by the Holy One, and <u>you</u> all*
   have knowledge.

Also reference 1 John 4.

1 John 4:4-6

---

[12] Michael L. Brown, *Hyper-Grace*, Charisma House, 2014, page 51, as he quotes Paul Ellis from his book, *The Gospel in Ten Words*, page 28.

4   *Little children, <u>you</u> are from God and have overcome **them**, for he who is in <u>you</u> is greater than he who is in the world.*

5   ***They** are from the world; therefore **they** speak from the world, and the world listens to **them**.*

6   *<u>We</u> are from God. Whoever knows God listens to <u>us</u>; whoever is not from God does not listen to <u>us</u>. By this we know the Spirit of truth and the spirit of error.*

Notice the difference between we/us and they/them. It couldn't be any plainer...the "we" is believers and the "they" are those outside the faith. So in 1 John 1:9, *If **we** confess **our** sins, he is faithful and just to forgive **us our** sins and to cleanse **us** from all unrighteousness*, the "we" is believers. We must dispense with this silly idea that "we" in 1 John 1:9 is not applied to Christ-followers.[13]

Additionally, the verb "confess" here is present tense which speaks NOT of a one-time act in the past, but of ongoing action. We don't keep confessing for the same sin, but we confess sin as we commit them. If, like Hyper-grace teachers state, that we are already forgiven for all future sins anyhow, why does James 5:15, which is written to believers, read the way it does?

James 5:14-15

*Is anyone among you sick? Let them call the elders of the church to pray over them and anoint them with oil in the name of the Lord. And the prayer offered in faith will make the sick person well; the Lord will raise them up. **If they have sinned, they will be forgiven.** (NIV)*

Wait...I thought this believer was already forgiven! Why would this believer need to be forgiven if he or she was forgiven

---

[13] Points here adapted from *Hyper-Grace*, Dr. Michael L. Brown, Charisma House, 2014, Chapter 5 – *Should Believers Confess Their Sins to God?*

2,000 years ago at the cross? The argument fails. (I'll touch on this again in Chapter 21, *The Fear of the Lord*)

But moving on...in order to confess our sin, we must be aware of our sin. We have a continuum with one end being sensitive to sin and the other being callous to it. The more we grow spiritually the more we move toward being sensitive when we have sinned and displeased God. This results in confession and repentance.

The opposite is when we have become insensitive to sin, or calloused to it.

Ephesians 4:19

*They have become **callous** (NIV – lost all sensitivity) and have given themselves up to sensuality, greedy to practice every kind of impurity.*

A callous is place of insensitivity. You can prick a callous with a pin and you don't feel pain when normally you would. But a truly born again person who is growing spiritually will have a new, tender heart—the old hard heart being removed in Christ.

Ezekiel 36:26

And I will give you a new heart, and a new spirit I will put within you. And I will remove the heart of stone from your flesh and give you a heart of flesh.

A new heart is a sign of true conversion. A hard heart indicates something is wrong. Are our hearts pricked when we sin and transgress God's commandments? Do we express genuine repentance when we do sin?

Here I'm referring to actual sin and not to culturally or socially defined things that are not necessarily sin according to God's Word. Shortly after I was born again, the movie *The Cross and the Switchblade* (1970) was showing in theaters. There was a pastor that I knew well that was very reluctant to see this movie with the rest of us because he grew up being told all movies and movie theaters were sinful. It wasn't a sin to go see this movie at a theater, but his own heart (not the Holy Spirit), condemned him. His heart condemned him but my heart didn't condemn me—all based on how we grew up.

1 John 3:19-21

*By this we shall know that we are of the truth and reassure our heart before him; for whenever **our heart condemns us**, God is greater than our heart, and he knows everything. Beloved, **if our heart does not condemn us**, we have confidence before God;*

One person's heart condemned them, another person's heart didn't, and all for the same exact thing. Sometimes this is caused by culturally ingrained conditioning. But this nuance does NOT apply to things that are plainly and objectively named sin in God's Word.

When we sin, we should feel "conviction" and its associated "guilt". Conviction and guilt are good things, contrary to what the world tells us. "Conviction" is when the Holy Spirit causes us to be aware when we have sinned and transgressed God's laws. It is the Holy Spirit enabling us to see things as God sees them. In talking about the soon coming Spirit, Jesus talked about what the Holy Spirit will do.

John 16:8

And when he (the Holy Spirit) comes, he will convict the world concerning sin and righteousness and judgment.

The Holy Spirit touches or "pricks" our conscience when we sin.

Romans 2:15

Their conscience also bears witness, and their conflicting thoughts accuse or even excuse them.

"Guilt" is the sense of blame we feel as a result of the Holy Spirit's conviction.

Psalm 38:4

My guilt has overwhelmed me like a burden too heavy to bear. (NIV)

Psalm 51:3

For I know my transgressions, and my sin is ever before me.

Conviction and guilt are good. But we need to differentiate between *conviction* and *condemnation*. *Conviction* is of the Holy Spirit and leads us to repentance (Romans 2:4 - *God's kindness is meant to lead you to repentance*). It is "godly sorrow" (2 Corinthians 7:10). *Condemnation*, on the other hand, is not from the Holy Spirit but from the devil and is intended to weigh a person down so that they never experience a sense of forgiveness. It is meant to tear down, to burden them down so that they don't feel a release of sin even though they've repented. That is not from God.

Romans 8:1

*There is therefore now **no condemnation** for those who are in Christ Jesus.*

We also need to differentiate between *real guilt* and *false guilt*. *Real guilt* is from God and comes when we violate His commandments. *False guilt* comes in two ways, first, if we sense guilt for things that are not really sins in the first place; and second, if we sense guilt for sin we have already confessed and repented of. In that case, the guilt is coming directly from Satan to paralyze us and tear us down.

Revelation 12:10

*For **the accuser** of our brothers has been thrown down, who **accuses them day and night** before our God*

This is talking about Satan, the "accuser," who continually assails against our minds for things that either aren't sins or sins we've already repented of.

The point here is, barring condemnation and false guilt, true believers should have a sensitivity to sin and be quick to confess and repent. A lack of this sensitivity to sin, a lack of "blushing" over sin (Jeremiah 6:15), would be a problem and indicate the person may not be born again, even though they profess to believe in Jesus Christ.

4. We keep God's commandments.

131

1 John 2:3-4

*And by this we know that **we have come to know him**, **if we keep his commandments**. Whoever says "I know him" but does not keep his commandments is a liar, and the truth is not in him.*

Those who **don't** keep His commandments **don't** know Him, even if they profess that they do. The sincere intentions and efforts of those truly born again are to obey God's commandments—to do what He says in His Word. Obeying God is important to those who are truly born again, and is reflected in their lifestyle choices.

1 John 3:2

Whoever keeps his commandments abides in God.

1 John 5:3

For this is the love of God, that we keep his commandments.

Jesus made this clear when He was here on the earth in His public ministry.

John 14:15

If you love me, you will keep my commandments.

Here we see a direct correlation between being born again (those who love Christ) and works (keeping His commandments). As a reminder, we're not saved by our good works, but if it's a true faith, good works (keeping the commandments) will be the result—the fruit.

James 2:18

I will show you my faith by my good deeds. (NLT)

A genuine faith will have corresponding obedience to God's commandments. Faith is not just believing, it's obeying.

2 Thessalonians 1:7-8

*When the Lord Jesus is revealed from heaven with his mighty angels in flaming fire, inflicting vengeance on those who do not know God and on **those who do not obey the gospel of our Lord Jesus.***

I find it interesting that it doesn't say God's judgment will fall on "those who do not BELIEVE the gospel of our Lord Jesus," it says it will fall on "those who DO NOT OBEY the gospel of our Lord Jesus." We tend to connect our relationship to the gospel with one of *believing*, but here the connection is *obeying*. That's why Romans 1:5 is phrased the way it is.

Romans 1:5

*Through whom we have received grace and apostleship to bring about **the obedience of faith** for the sake of his name among all the nations.*

It doesn't say "the believing of faith," it says "the obedience of faith." We see this again later in the book of Romans.

Romans 16:26

*But has now been disclosed and through the prophetic writings has been made known to all nations, according to the command of the eternal God, to bring about **the obedience of faith**.*

What God desires to bring about is not the "believing of faith," but "the obedience of faith." Believing the gospel intellectually doesn't cut it. Genuine faith will result in obedience to the gospel, and this is one of the marks that the Apostle John points out as one of the things whereby we can know whether we have eternal life or not.

1 John 2:3-4

*And by this we know that **we have come to know him, if we keep his commandments**. Whoever says "I know him" but does not keep his commandments is a liar, and the truth is not in him.*

To examine myself, I must ask questions:

- Do I have a desire to obey God's commandments, or do I ignore them?
- When I see one of God's commandments in Scripture, do I think about how I'm doing in that area? Do I think about how I can obey that commandment in better ways?
- How do I react when I see a commandment that I don't like? Do I try to rationalize it away?
- Do I delight in knowing and obeying God's commands?

Psalm 119:47

I find my delight in your commandments, which I love.

5. We love people...all people. We are known to be kind, loving people.

1 John 2:10

Whoever loves his brother abides in the light, and in him there is no cause for stumbling.

The Apostle John identifies love as one of the most critical indicators of someone who is vitally connected to God through Jesus Christ. Read and sense the full impact of the next verse.

1 John 3:14

We know that we have passed out of death into life, because we love the brothers. Whoever does not love abides in death.

That's pretty straightforward. Someone who is living in bitterness, hatred and unforgiveness is not someone who is living in Christ, even if they profess that they are. Loving others is a key indicator of being a true follower of Jesus Christ.

John 13:35

By this all people will know that you are my disciples, if you have love for one another.

Is our church known for being loving? Am I? Someone may inquire, "Well how do I know?" The Apostle Paul helped us out with this.

1 Corinthians 13:4-6

Love is patient and kind. Love is not jealous or boastful or proud or rude. It does not demand its own way. It is not irritable, and it keeps no record of being wronged. It does not rejoice about injustice but rejoices whenever the truth wins out. (NLT)

If married, ask your spouse (if not married, ask a best friend or family member):

- Am I patient and kind?
- Am I jealous, boastful or proud?
- Am I rude to people?
- Do I demand my own way a lot?
- Am I irritable?
- Do I keep a record of wrongs done to me?
- Do I rejoice when someone I don't like takes a fall or is taken advantage of?

How did you fare on that test? The key to walking in love toward others is understanding that love, infinite love, already dwells on the inside of us IF we're sincere followers of Jesus Christ.

1 John 4:16

God is love, *and whoever abides in love abides in God, and* **God abides in him.**

God lives on the inside of us, and He is love!

Romans 5:5

God's love has been poured into our hearts *through the Holy Spirit who has been given to us.*

If you're a sincere follower of Christ, you cannot say, "I just don't have love inside me." That would not be true. You may not be *releasing* that love, but Scripture guarantees that if we're disciples, if we're genuine followers of Jesus Christ, the love of God has been poured into us by the Holy Spirit. Now it's a matter of releasing that love and giving it expression.

1 John 3:23

And this is his commandment, that we believe in the name of his Son Jesus Christ and love one another, just as he has commanded us.

The Apostle John is known as *the Apostle of love*. It's not hard to see why, as you'll see from this passage.

1 John 4:7-12

7   *Beloved, let us love one another, for love is from God, and whoever loves has been born of God and knows God.*

8   *Anyone who does not love does not know God, because God is love.*

9   *In this the love of God was made manifest among us, that God sent his only Son into the world, so that we might live through him.*

10 *In this is love, not that we have loved God but that he loved us and sent his Son to be the propitiation for our sins.*

11 *Beloved, if God so loved us, we also ought to love one another.*

12 *No one has ever seen God; if we love one another, God abides in us and his love is perfected in us.*

One thing we have to resist in giving ourselves high marks in the area of love, is when only scoring ourselves on how we love our favorite family members, friends and co-workers. Jesus had something to say about that.

Luke 6:32

If you love those who love you, what benefit is that to you? For even sinners love those who love them.

So the true test is not how we love those we naturally love anyhow. The true test is how we love and treat those who are difficult to love, those who irritate us.

We must also use caution so that we don't restrict our definition of love to that which is just warm and fuzzy. Certainly affection and kind words are a big part of love. But sometimes love expresses itself in ways which would be considered as direct and straight, sometimes even hard. In Matthew 16:23 Jesus called Peter "Satan." I've said some hard things before, but I've never called someone Satan. I may have thought it, but I didn't say it. Yet, as with everything Jesus did, it was done in love.

A lady in a desperate situation came to Jesus one time and pleaded with Him to heal her daughter who was demon possessed. How did Jesus' love express itself with this lady?

Matthew 15:26

And he answered, "It is not right to take the children's bread and throw it to the dogs."

Ouch! I've said some hard things before, but I've never called someone a dog. I may have thought it, but I didn't say it. But even here Jesus said it in love, because He intentionally wanted her to get a little angry so that she would rise up in faith to receive for her daughter.

Matthew 15:27-28

She said, "Yes, Lord, yet even the dogs eat the crumbs that fall from their masters' table." Then Jesus answered her, "O woman, great is your faith! Be it done for you as you desire." And her daughter was healed instantly.

Jesus said some tough things. One time a guy came up and wanted to follow Jesus but asked if he could first go bury his father who had just died. How was Jesus' love for the man expressed?

Matthew 8:22

And Jesus said to him, "Follow me, and leave the dead to bury their own dead."

Are you kidding? The man's father just died! But this was still an act of love, Jesus intentionally making the man understand the cost of discipleship, and that following Jesus comes before everything else. Sometimes love is direct.

137

Proverbs 27:5,6

Better is open rebuke than hidden love. Faithful are the wounds of a friend; profuse are the kisses of an enemy.

Yes, sometimes love rebukes and wounds, but it's out of a heart of love, and is meant for godly transformation. Love is not always warm and fuzzy. But whether love is expressed as soft or sometimes hard, the mark of a true Christ-follower is that they are known to be kind, loving people.

Chapter 14

Evidence for Faith – Part 2

As a reminder, we are told in Scripture to examine and test ourselves to ensure that we are in the faith, that is, truly saved or born again.

2 Corinthians 13:5

Examine yourselves, to see whether you are in the faith. Test yourselves. Or do you not realize this about yourselves, that Jesus Christ is in you?—unless indeed you fail to meet the test!

2 Peter 1:10

Therefore, brothers, be all the more diligent to confirm your calling and election, for if you practice these qualities you will never fall.

Additionally, we are given criteria to help us determine whether we are "in the faith."

1 John 5:13

I write these things to you who believe in the name of the Son of God, that you may know that you have eternal life.

Therefore we should look at the things written in 1 John to help us determine whether we ha–ve eternal life or not. In 1 John, we find ten indicators that can assist us in examining and testing ourselves to see if we have eternal life and are born again. In our last chapter, we listed five evidences for possessing a genuine faith:

1. Fellowship with the Father, Son and other believers.
2. We walk in the light (holiness) and choose not to walk in darkness (sin).
3. We are sensitive to our sin and God's conviction of it. We are quick to confess and repent.
4. We keep God's commandments.
5. We love people...all people. We are known to be kind, loving people.

We must examine ourselves to see how we're doing in these areas. We'll never score 100% on all these points, but those truly born again will exhibit these evidences and will certainly be making deliberate progress in these areas. In this chapter, because it's a major point that needs explaining and is worth a closer look, we'll just cover the next evidence for faith.

6. We avoid worldly affections and don't allow ourselves to be shaped by the world.

1 John 2:15-16

Do not love the world or the things in the world. If anyone loves the world, the love of the Father is not in him. For all that is in the world—the desires of the flesh and the desires of the eyes and pride of life—is not from the Father but is from the world.

2 Timothy 4:9-10

*Do your best to come to me soon. For Demas, **in love with this present world**, has deserted me and gone to Thessalonica.*

One thing that delineates Christ-followers from unbelievers is the degree of their attachment to this world. It touches on both their affections as well as the degree their thinking is molded by culture, or what we sometimes call *zeitgeist*. Zeitgeist (German: *zeit* = time, and *geist* = ghost or spirit), is *the spirit of the times*. To what degree has *zeitgeist*, the spirit of the times or the spirit of the world, rubbed off onto or into believers' thinking and behavior?

This doesn't mean Christ-followers never think about worldly things. They do that daily. But it does mean that Christ-followers don't get *entangled* with worldly things that distract them from full devotion to Christ.

2 Timothy 2:4

*No soldier **gets entangled** in civilian pursuits, since his aim is to please the one who enlisted him.*

Touching something and getting entangled in it are two different things. It means we don't set our affections on worldly things. It means we are not shaped or molded by worldly thinking, at least the ungodly aspects of that thinking.

Someone may ask, "But wait...John 3:16 says that "**God so loved the world**, that He gave His only begotten Son." God loves the world but we're not supposed to?"

The word "world" in Greek (from which the New Testament was written), is *kosmos*, and is defined three different ways in Scripture:

1. The physical world and universe.
2. The inhabitants of the world.
3. Worldly systems, culture and thinking.

In John 3:16, "God so loved the *world*," definition 2 applies, *the inhabitants of the world*. However, here in 1 John 2:15-16, "love not the *world* or the things in *world*," it refers to definition 3, *worldly systems, culture and thinking*. You can see this in 1 John 2:16, "the desires of the flesh, the desires of the eyes, the pride of life." This is talking about carnal appetites, ungodly thinking and activities, ungodly aspects of the culture. All those things attract mankind's devotion away from full, unfettered devotion to Christ.

There are two main ways this can happen. One can be worldly by *omission* or *commission*. **Worldly by omission** means the individual omits actively loving and living for God as evidenced by behaviors consistent with full devotion to Christ. A person can be involved with legitimate things—their career, relationships, hobbies and recreation; but they rarely pray, worship God, study and meditate upon Scripture, regularly attend and volunteer in a church, share Christ with other people, give financially into the kingdom of God, or follow God's commandments. The things they're involved with are not sinful necessarily, it's just that they have omitted engaging in what are called "the spiritual disciplines."[14]

Worldly by commission means actively engaging in carnal thinking or activities that are contrary to Scripture and godliness.

There are five things that indicate that something has moved from being a legitimate concern, affection or activity, to a worldly and ungodly one:

1. Kind (sinful or not as defined by Scripture)
2. Time (how much time given to it)
3. Frequency (how often it's engaged in)
4. Degree (degree of intensity and involvement)
5. Effect (the effect it has on the person's thinking and behavior)

For number 1, *kind*, there are some things that are unquestionably wrong as defined by Scripture, no matter who you are, what country you live in or what period of time. But there are other things that aren't inherently sin, but could become sin depending on time, frequency, degree and effect.

For example, let's take fun and recreation, which are good and lead to a balanced, holistic life. God didn't intend for us to work all the time, be serious all the time or be bored. God designed us to enjoy life.

1 Timothy 6:17

*As for the rich in this present age, charge them not to be haughty, nor to set their hopes on the uncertainty of riches, but on **God, who richly provides us with everything to enjoy**.*

God's not against us enjoying His creation and having fun. He created a wonderful world to enjoy and gave mankind the capacity to create, dream, play, laugh and enjoy each other in fun activities.

Ecclesiastes 2:24

---

14   For further study: *The Spirit of the Disciples* (Dallas Willard), *Celebration of Discipline* (Richard Foster), *The Life You've Always Wanted* (John Ortberg).

*So I decided there is nothing better than to enjoy food and drink and to find satisfaction in work. Then I realized that **these pleasures are from the hand of God**. (NLT)*

God's not against pleasure. Asceticism (avoidance of all pleasure) is contrary to God's design and will for His children.

Psalm 16:11

*You make known to me the path of life; in your presence there is **fullness of joy**; at your right hand are **pleasures forevermore**.*

And yet, a legitimate thing can become wrong at a certain point, IF it takes too much time and devotion, displacing rightful time and devotion to Christ.

1 Corinthians 10:23

"All things are lawful," but not all things are helpful (NIV – beneficial). "All things are lawful," but not all things build up (NIV – not everything is constructive).

We should interpret "helpful" and "beneficial" here as relating to spiritual growth and godliness.

1 Corinthians 6:12

"All things are lawful for me," but not all things are helpful. "All things are lawful for me," but I will not be dominated by anything.

We see a glimpse of *frequency*, *degree* and *intensity* here with the phrase, "I will not be dominated by anything." That's a pretty good test. If something lawful and legitimate escalates to the point of dominating our time, money and interest, it's wrong. If the activity is not constructive and beneficial to you, if it draws you away from Christ and holy living, then it is wrong.

I know a man in the one of churches I pastored who came to church weekly. He believed in and professed Christ. When one of our elders encouraged him to engage in the daily spiritual disciplines (exercises) of Bible reading, meditation and prayer, he said he didn't have time because he got up early and did his rigorous exercise routine before work. Because he owned a business, he was there all day and when he got home, he was tired and just wanted to relax. Is exercise legitimate? Yes. Is career legitimate? Yes. Is relaxing legitimate? Yes. But when exercise, career and relaxing dominate you to the point that you have no time to pray, read and meditate on Scripture or worship, there's something wrong. At that point, you have "loved the world and the things in the world." Legitimate activities morphed into sin. It's Christ and His kingdom that come first for genuine Christ-followers.

Matthew 6:33

> But **seek first the kingdom of God** and his righteousness, and all these things will be added to you.

Colossians 1:18

> And he is the head of the body, the church; he is the beginning and the firstborn from among the dead, so that **in everything he might have the supremacy.** (NIV)

Psalm 73:25-26

> Whom have I in heaven but you? And **there is nothing on earth that I desire besides you.** My flesh and my heart may fail, but God is the strength of my heart and my portion forever.

Philippians 3:7-8

> But whatever gain I had, I counted as loss for the sake of Christ. Indeed, **I count everything as loss because of the surpassing worth of knowing Christ Jesus my Lord.**

Everything else must pale in comparison to knowing, worshipping, serving and following Jesus Christ.

With Christ-followers, the desire for earthly things takes a back seat, and for three reasons. First, because, as already mentioned, Christ comes first. Second, because everything in this world is temporary and will eventually burn up.

1 John 2:17

And the world is passing away along with its desires, but whoever does the will of God abides forever.

Third, as Christ-followers, we must understand that we are foreigners and aliens in this world. We're just passing through and shouldn't get too attached to it.

Hebrews 11:13

*Having acknowledged that they were **strangers and exiles on the earth**.*

Philippians 3:20

But our citizenship is in heaven. *And we eagerly await a Savior from there, the Lord Jesus Christ,*

1 Peter 2:11

*Dear friends, I warn you as **"temporary residents and foreigners"** to keep away from worldly desires that wage war against your very souls.*

Notice the connection between knowing we're *temporary residents and foreigners* and distancing ourselves from worldly desires. Notice also that these worldly desires *wage war against our souls*. This is not talking about legitimate worldly desires, it's referring to that which is ungodly and draws us away from Christ.

I want to make this very clear...worldly desires wage a war against our souls, against our full devotion to Christ and spiritual growth. And again, these desires can be legitimate things taken to a time/frequency/degree that take precedent over devotion to Christ. There's nothing sinful about owning a boat, but if one is on the boat so often that it causes them to regularly miss church and assembling with other believers, then a legitimate thing has become sin in the sense that they have let a worldly desire dominate them (1 Corinthians 6:12).

Hebrews 10:25

And let us not neglect our meeting together, as some people do.

Criteria point 5 in determining whether something has morphed from legitimate to worldly, is "effect." By "effect" we mean the effect that it has on the believer's thinking and behavior. Does that TV program, movie, website, book, hobby, or activity with friends draw you away from godliness, devotion to Christ and holy living? Getting back to a question posed earlier, to what degree has *zeitgeist* rubbed off onto or into believers' thinking and behavior?

1 John 2:15-16 means that those who are truly born again don't think or behave like the world. Listen to this command from Romans 12.

Romans 12:2

Don't copy the behavior and customs of this world, but let God transform you into a new person by changing the way you think. (NLT)

Romans 12:2

Don't let the world around you squeeze you into its own mold, but let God remold your minds from within. (PME)

This is a huge problem for Christians because many have allowed worldly, ungodly thinking to affect them. They have been squeezed into the world's mold instead of being transformed by allowing God to remold their thinking and behavior.

For example, let's take Christians' views of homosexuality. A 2015 Pew Research poll reported that 54% of Christians believed that homosexuality "should be accepted, rather than discouraged, by society."[15] Although percentages vary by denomination, the same organization reported that 62% of white mainline protestants favor gay marriage.[16] This shows that many Christians stand with the world instead of Jesus Christ, although of course they would deny this. The world celebrates and extols homosexuality and gay marriage as part of "love." Our nation's president lit up the White House with rainbow colors to celebrate

---

[15] http://www.pewresearch.org/fact-tank/2015/12/18/most-u-s-christian-groups-grow-more-accepting-of-homosexuality/

[16] http://www.pewresearch.org/fact-tank/2015/12/21/where-christian-churches-stand-on-gay-marriage/

the Supreme Court's decision to legalize gay marriage. What does God think?

Luke 16:15

What this world honors is detestable in the sight of God. (NLT)

Both the Old and New Testaments clearly and unambiguously condemn homosexuality as sin, yet many Christians have allowed the world's thinking rub off on them and take precedent over what God says. Jesus quoted the Old Testament and reiterated in the New Testament that marriage is between a man and woman (Genesis 2:24 and Matthew 19:5). Yet, Christians will succumb to culture and ungodly thinking by embracing a different definition of marriage. They side with the world instead of siding with Jesus Christ.

When someone sides with culture over God, they have become friends with the world.

1 John 2:15

If anyone loves the world, the love of the Father is not in him.

Another area where Christians embrace zeitgeist, the spirit of the world, is with divorce. There are scriptural reasons permitting divorce, but incompatibility is not one of them. As I survey all the couples I have performed marriages for in my career as a pastor, a shocking number of them are divorced. This grieves me and certainly grieves the heart of God. Christians divorce for the same reasons that the world divorces—arguing, not seeing eye-to-eye, incompatibility, viewing life differently, wanting to take a different life direction, and preference for a different kind of spouse, that "special someone." Well guess what? That doesn't cut it with God! If this has been the case with you, repent, and if you have already repented, then you are forgiven. But this point had to be mentioned because it's an area where Christians have become friends with the world. And God doesn't wink at this sin.

James 4:4

*You adulterous people! Do you not know that **friendship with the world is enmity with God**? Therefore whoever wishes to be a friend of the world makes himself an enemy of God.*

We're either friends with the world or friends with God, one or the other, but not both. Genuine believers mustn't be friends with the world because the world's system of thinking and behaving is influenced by Satan himself.

John 14:30

*I will no longer talk much with you, for **the ruler of this world** is coming. He has no claim on me*

Someone may say, "Well Tom, that was before the cross and resurrection. Satan is no longer the ruler of this world, God is." Although that sounds right, it's not true. Here's Scripture written long after the cross and resurrection.

1 John 5:19

*We know that we are from God, and **the whole world lies in the power of the evil one.***

2 Corinthians 4:4

*In their case **the god of this world** has blinded the minds of the unbelievers, to keep them from seeing the light of the gospel of the glory of Christ, who is the image of God.*

The spirit behind the world and its systems is the devil. But Jesus died to deliver us from ungodly worldly thinking and behavior.

Galatians 1:3-4

*The Lord Jesus Christ, who gave himself for our sins **to deliver us from the present evil age.***

Christ did this so that we would be set free from being influenced by "the god of this world," and no longer follow worldly desires.

Ephesians 2:1-3

1   And you were dead in the trespasses and sins

2   *in which you once walked, following the course of this world, following the prince of the power of the air, the spirit that is now at work in the sons of disobedience—*

3   *among whom we all once lived in **the passions of our flesh, carrying out the desires of the body and the mind,** and were by nature children of wrath, like the rest of mankind.*

Before we were Christians we used to "follow the course of this world," we used to "live in the passions of the flesh," we used to "carry out the desires of the body and mind." After being born again it's supposed to be different. If it's the same, something is seriously wrong.

We become friends with the world when our thinking and behavior becomes like that of the world and contrary to godliness and holiness. We become friends with the world when we allow its thinking to get on us, to affect us.

2 Peter 2:20

*If they have escaped **the corruption (KJV – pollutions) of the world** by knowing our Lord and Savior Jesus Christ and are again entangled in it and are overcome, they are worse off at the end than they were at the beginning.*

Those who are born again have escaped *the corruption (pollutions) of the world* by knowing Christ. Having done so, we are to think and act differently. We must take this evidence from 1 John 2:15 for being born again seriously.

1 John 2:15

Do not love the world or the things in the world. *If anyone loves the world, the love of the Father is not in him.*

Spiritual growth, after being born again, means we say no to worldly thinking and behaving. We allow the Holy Spirit to transform us (Romans 12:2 – *Be transformed by the renewing of your mind*). But at its core, we must understand that ongoing worldly affections and behavior indicate that something is wrong spiritually. There's something wrong in the relationship with God.

Romans 8:7

> *For the mind that is set on the flesh (carnal, worldly thinking) is hostile to God, for it does not submit to God's law; indeed, it cannot.*

Either the person was never saved in the first place, or they have backslidden away from God and need to return to Him. The answer is to understand what it truly means to receive Jesus as "Lord."

Chapter 15

Evidence for Faith – Part 3

Jesus stated in Matthew 7:21-23, that on judgment day (refer to Revelation 20:11-15), **many** people will call Him Lord, but He will respond, "I never knew you, you who do lawlessness." Jesus used the word "**many**." This means there are **many**, not a few, but **many** people who think they're saved, but really aren't. On the day of judgement, **many** people will expect to hear from God, "Well done, good and faithful servant. You have been faithful over a little; I will set you over much. Enter into the joy of your master (Matthew 25:21)," but will instead hear, "I never knew you; depart from me, you workers of lawlessness (Matthew 7:23)." This is troubling. This should cause us to look at the dynamics of why this is and remedy it.

Sadly, this is seldom preached. When was the time you heard a sermon about this? The reason you don't hear it preached is because of BIS. BIS is "bodies in seats." Pastors need bodies in seats, and therefore are very careful not to preach things that would turn people away. If they ever do preach on these things it's so watered down that the people in the seats just don't get it.

Jesus also taught that we'll be able to recognize those who are truly His, and those who aren't. He said in Matthew 7:16, "You will recognize them by their fruits." If Jesus didn't want us to recognize or discern who were truly His and those who weren't, why did He say that? He said, "A healthy tree cannot bear bad fruit, nor can a diseased tree bear good fruit (Matthew 7:18)." *Fruit* here is talking about behavior and conduct. Then Jesus made a startling statement in Matthew 7:19, "Every tree that does not bear good fruit is cut down and thrown into the fire." This corresponds with four verses later, verse 23, "I never knew you; depart from me, you workers of lawlessness."

It begs the question, "How does one know whether their fruit lines up with their profession of faith?" After all, we are commanded in 2 Corinthians 13:5, "Examine yourselves, to see whether you are in the faith. Test yourselves." Where can we find this test? Previously we've seen that the Apostle John gave us criteria for helping us ascertain the evidence for being saved.

1 John 5:13

I write these things to you who believe in the name of the Son of God, that you may know that you have eternal life.

Therefore, we can take a good look at the letter of 1 John to see the evidence that he identifies. So far, we've listed six things which give strong evidence that someone is truly born again:

1. Fellowship with the Father, Son and other believers.
2. We walk in the light (holiness) and choose not to walk in darkness (sin).
3. We are sensitive to our sin and God's conviction of it. We are quick to confess and repent.
4. We keep God's commandments.
5. We love people...all people. We are known to be kind, loving people.
6. We avoid worldly affections and don't allow ourselves to be shaped by the world.

In this chapter, we'll show the last four evidences from the book of 1 John for someone being born again and possessing eternal life.

7. We openly believe and confess our relationship with Christ.

1 John 5:1

*Everyone who **believes** that Jesus is the Christ has been born of God.*

1 John 2:23

*Whoever **confesses** the Son has the Father also.*

1 John 4:15

*Whoever **confesses** that Jesus is the Son of God, God abides in him, and he in God.*

One evidence that someone is truly saved is that they openly believe and confess Jesus Christ as their Lord and Savior. They are not incognito believers. Family, friends, neighbors and co-workers know them to be Christ-followers.

"Confessing" Christ is done in three ways:
1. Initial – at the time of receiving Christ.
2. Ongoing – regularly after that.
3. Publicly – to others.

If we take these verses from 1 John in harmony with the rest of Scripture, we'll understand confessing Christ is not to be just a private thing, but a public expression as well. No public profession of Christ would be suspect, and indicate a problem in the relationship with the Lord.

Matthew 10:32-33

*So everyone who **acknowledges** (NASB – **confesses**) me before men, I also will acknowledge before my Father who is in heaven, but whoever denies me before men, I also will deny before my Father who is in heaven.*

Those truly born again cannot be silent about Christ. There is a threefold reason for this. First, we are commanded to share the gospel with others (Matthew 28:19-20). Secondly, just like if one discovered the cure for cancer, we should be eager to share the good news of the gospel with others so they too can also receive freedom from the bondage of sin and its consequence, along with inheriting eternal life.

2 Corinthians 5:14

For Christ's love compels us, because we are convinced that one died for all, and therefore all died. (NIV)

Thirdly, there is a biblical principle which states that if something is truly inside of us, it will eventually come out.

Matthew 12:34

For out of the abundance of the heart the mouth speaks.

2 Corinthians 4:13

Since we have the same spirit of faith according to what has been written, "I believed, and so I spoke," we also believe, and so we also speak,

If someone is filled with Christ, they will confess Him to others. This doesn't mean they'll share Christ with everyone they meet. It doesn't mean they'll be obnoxious and "bible-belt" people. But it does mean they will share Christ and confess their relationship with Him to others in hopes they may come to know Him as their Lord and Savior as well.

If Jesus Christ is the most important thing (person) in our lives, would we not be talking about Him to others? You'd have to question someone who claims Jesus Christ is the most important person in their life but their family, friends, neighbors and co-workers have never heard that from them. If our whole life was oriented around volunteering in animal shelters, if that was the most important thing to us in the whole world, wouldn't people who know us be aware of that?

If our fiancé or spouse was the most important person in our life, if our day and week was ordered around spending time with them, wouldn't others we're close with know about that?

8. We demonstrate God's love by meeting the needs of others.

1 John 3:17-18

But if anyone has the world's goods and sees his brother in need, yet closes his heart against him, how does God's love abide in him? Little children, let us not love in word or talk but in deed and in truth.

When those who were previously selfish and self-absorbed become born again and transformed by the Holy Spirit, they become aware of others' needs and have an open hand. They become giving people. This may include money, physical goods, time, love and encouraging words (Proverbs 15:23 – "To make an apt answer is a joy to a man, and a word in season, how good it is!"). Christ-followers become like Christ.

1 John 4:17

*By this is love perfected with us, so that we may have confidence for the day of judgment, because **as he is so also are we in this world**.*

Notice the connection between love in us and acting like Jesus in this world. And how did Jesus act in this world?

Matthew 15:32

Then Jesus called his disciples to him and said, "I have compassion on the crowd because they have been with me now three days and have nothing to eat. And I am unwilling to send them away hungry, lest they faint on the way."

What did Jesus do? He fed them. I call this "the eye-heart-hand" connection. Jesus saw the crowds and their need (eye), He was moved with compassion (heart), then met the need (hand). And… "as he is so also are we in this world."

Those truly born again are givers, they meet the needs of others. Sometimes that comes in the form of money, sometimes giving away physical goods, and sometimes it comes in the form of volunteering their time to serve the needy, say in a food pantry or soup kitchen. Sometimes they get off the couch and help people move when aware of someone needing that kind of assistance. I've tried to use helping people move as a litmus test of love in my own life. If aware of someone moving and needing help, do I wait to be asked or do I initiate a call to them and volunteer?

Meeting needs was one of the first signs of Christians loving one another.

Acts 2:44-45

And all who believed were together and had all things in common. And they were selling their possessions and belongings and distributing the proceeds to all, as any had need.

For a book that will stir your heart and challenge your thinking, I recommend: *The Hole in the Gospel – What Does God Expect of Us?* - by Richard Stearns.[17] The book is primarily geared toward a global view, but the principles apply locally.

9. We listen and pay attention to sound instruction from God's Word through others.

1 John 4:6

*We are from God. **Whoever knows God listens to us**; whoever is not from God does not listen to us. By this we know the Spirit of truth and the spirit of error.*

The main way we discern spiritual truth from error is when we listen to God-appointed, God-anointed teachers of His Word, what this verse calls someone "from God." All believers in Christ could and should read Scripture for themselves...daily. But we should also regularly listen to those whom God has called and equipped to teach sound doctrine. For believers, this primarily means sitting under good teaching in a local church.

In Acts 2, after Peter's sermon which resulted in thousands of people believing and accepting Christ as their Messiah, the first thing believers did was connect with other believers and sit under teaching.

Acts 2:41-42

*So those who received his word were baptized, and there were added that day about three thousand souls. And they **devoted themselves to the apostles' teaching** and the fellowship, to the breaking of bread and the prayers.*

Receiving regular teaching from God's Word through men and women whom God has called and anointed to teach, is a key mark of a genuine follower of Christ. God set these teachers in the church to teach, shepherd and equip believers and lead them in the furtherance of their spiritual growth. Notice in this passage from Ephesians 4 the role those called by God to lead, teach and

---

[17]   The Hole in the Gospel – What Does God Expect of us? – Richard Stearns, 2010, Thomas Nelson

shepherd God's people play, and how believers are designed to come together as a body, the church.

Ephesians 4:11-16

11 *And he gave the apostles, the prophets, the evangelists, the shepherds and teachers, (why?)*

12 *to equip the saints for the work of ministry, for building up the body of Christ,*

13 *until we all attain to the unity of the faith and of the knowledge of the Son of God, **to mature manhood**, to the measure of the stature of the fullness of Christ,*

14 *so that we may no longer be children, tossed to and fro by the waves and carried about by every wind of doctrine, by human cunning, by craftiness in deceitful schemes.*

15 *Rather, speaking the truth in love, we are **to grow up** in every way into him who is the head, into Christ,*

16 *from whom the whole body, **joined and held together by every joint** with which it is equipped, when each part is working properly, **makes the body grow** so that it builds itself up in love.*

Verse 14 makes the same point as 1 John 4:6, that the reason God wants us to listen to teachers of His Word is so that we discern truth from error. Regularly receiving sound teaching is a key mark of a true disciple.

10. We put God first place in our lives. We guard ourselves from any person, thing or desire which tries to usurp God's rightful place as the most important thing in our lives.

1 John 5:21

*Little children, **keep yourselves from idols**.*

The word *keep* means *to guard*. An *idol* is any person, thing, affection or desire that rises in importance above our relationship with Jesus Christ. We are to guard ourselves from anything being more important than our relationship with Him.

If your spouse is more important than Christ, your spouse is an idol. If your children are more important than the ten points listed in these three chapters about evidence, your children are idols that take the place of God. If hunting, fishing, friends, family, boating, travelling, partying, movies, exercise, fashion, or your career are more important than these ten points, they are idols which have usurped God's rightful position in your life as Lord and God. The very first of the Ten Commandments is: "You shall have no other gods before Me." (Exodus 20:3; Deuteronomy 5:7)

How do we determine whether something is an idol? Answer:

1. Time.
   - How much time you spend on it.
   - If a person devotes more time to people and pleasures, but doesn't have time to devote to the spiritual disciplines and their walk with God, something is wrong.

2. Money.
   - How much you invest in it.
   - If a person doesn't tithe (tithe = 10%) but spends money on all their personal interests, something is wrong.

3. Degree of desire and affection.
   - How much you think about and desire it.
   - If a person thinks more about their desires, hobbies and interests more than yearning to know and follow Jesus Christ, something is wrong.

Any legitimate person, thing or desire can morph into an idol. 1 John 5:21 instructs us to guard ourselves from anything taking the place of being more important than God, through Christ.

Why did the Apostle John give us all these ten points?

1 John 5:13

I write these things to you who believe in the name of the Son of God, that you may know that you have eternal life.

He wrote them so we could examine ourselves to discern whether we have eternal life or not.

Are we going to hit a home run on every single one of these ten evidences? No. But there should be a general sense that we are making serious progress ("so that everyone may see your progress" – 1 Timothy 4:15) in these things and feel conviction when we aren't. And though there will be times of drifting away from the Lord or even downright seasons of backsliding into sin, if we take our entire lives as a whole after accepting Christ, do they reflect these ten elements for the most part?

In truth, we're all on a spiritual journey, and some are further along than others. If we could picture a continuum, it would look like this:

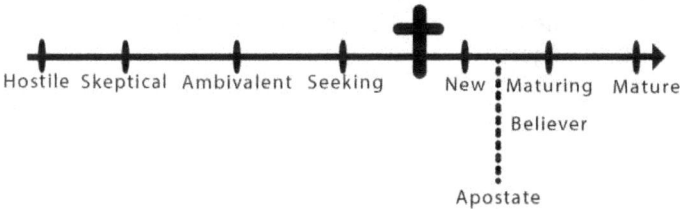

We want to continuously move to the right, to "Mature." Remember Ephesians 4:13, which defines the goal.

Ephesians 4:13

Until we all attain to the unity of the faith and of the knowledge of the Son of God, to mature manhood, to the measure of the stature of the fullness of Christ.

Here are our ten evidences from 1 John of being genuinely born again and having eternal life.

1. Fellowship with the Father, Son and other believers.
2. We walk in the light (holiness) and choose not to walk in darkness (sin).

159

3. We are sensitive to our sin and God's conviction of it. We are quick to confess and repent.
4. We keep God's commandments.
5. We love people...all people. We are known to be kind, loving people.
6. We avoid worldly affections and don't allow ourselves to be shaped by the world.
7. We openly believe and confess our relationship with Christ.
8. We demonstrate God's love by meeting the needs of others.
9. We listen and pay attention to sound instruction from God's Word through others.
10. We put God first place in our lives. We guard ourselves from any person, thing or desire which tries to usurp God's rightful place as the most important thing in our lives.

What if, after examining ourselves, we find we're not doing so well? The good news is—we can go back, laying hold of Christ anew, and begin following Him again daily.

At the root of a good spiritual foundation and born-again experience, is an understanding of who we are accepting and following in the first place. The next part of this book will tackle this critical subject.

CHAPTER 16

Jesus' Two-fold Offices

Finally, in this book we come to the crux of the matter...Lord and Savior. Down through biblical history God has always manifested Himself primarily through a two-fold nature, this nature finding its eventual earthly and visible expression through Jesus Christ, who was given these divine titles and offices. Everything God said or did (says or does), can be directly linked to one of these two aspects of His nature.

The two aspects of His nature, and therefore the two primary offices or titles that Jesus Christ stands in, are *Lord* and *Savior*.

This is not to say that Jesus doesn't have more titles than these two. He, in fact, has many. He is:

- The Messiah or Christ (John 1:41, Matthew 16:16, Matthew 26:63-64)
- The Alpha and Omega – The First and the Last (Revelation 1:17, Revelation 22:13)
- The Son of God (Matthew 14:33, Matthew 16:16, John 3:18)
- The Son of Man (Matthew 8:20, Matthew 9:6, Matthew 16:13)
- The Son of David (Matthew 20:30-31, Matthew 15:22, 2 Samuel 7:12-16, Romans 1:3)
- The Lamb of God (John 1:29, John 1:36, Revelation 5:6)
- The Last Adam (1 Corinthians 15:45-49)
- The Light of the World (John 8:12)
- The King of the Jews (Matthew 2:1-2, Matthew 27:37)
- The Word of God (John 1:1)
- The Lion of Judah (Revelation 5:5)
- The Amen (Revelation 3:14)
- The Bright Morning Star (Revelation 22:16, 2 Peter 1:19)
- The Seed of Abraham (Galatians 3:16)

- The Author and Perfecter of our faith (Hebrews 12:2)
- The Firstborn from the Dead (Revelation 1:5)
- The Head of the Church (Ephesians 1:22-23)
- The Bridegroom (John 3:29, Matthew 25:1-12 with Revelation 19:7)
- Immanuel (Matthew 1:23)
- The Passover Lamb (1 Corinthians 5:7)
- The Apostle and High Priest of our Confession (Hebrews 3:1)

However, when we look at the New Testament carefully, we see that *Lord* and *Savior* are His two primary titles. Everything else pings off these two.

2 Peter 1:11

*For in this way there will be richly provided for you an entrance into the eternal kingdom of our **Lord** and **Savior** Jesus Christ.*

The two main titles or offices He stands in are important and insightful. The titles are very different but both are descriptive of what actions emanate from them.

For example, the title "caregiver" would clue us in on what that person does, what position they hold and the purpose of that position. The title "law enforcement officer" would give a completely different idea. The nature of a law enforcement officer is much different than the nature of a caregiver. Similarly, the titles *Lord* and *Savior* describe the nature of those titles and offices. Though most Christians are well familiar with these titles, few know the full impact of them.

When God blesses, provides, protects, heals, answers prayer and delivers people, He's expressing His nature as **Savior**. When God gives commands, or acts in judgment when His commands aren't followed, He's expressing His nature as **Lord**. This theme of Lord and Savior runs throughout the entire Bible. It's actually very easy to spot which aspect of God's nature He's speaking or acting from.

Deuteronomy 6:1-2

Now this is the commandment—the statutes and the rules—that the Lord your God commanded me to teach you (commandment = Lord), that you may do them in the land to which you are going over, to possess it (blessing = Savior), that you may fear the Lord your God, you and your son and your son's son, by keeping all his statutes and his commandments, which I command you (commandment = Lord), all the days of your life, and that your days may be long (blessing = Savior).

When God issues commands, it springs from His nature as *Lord*. When God blesses, it issues from His nature as *Savior* (one who saves, heals, provides and delivers). The following chapters will explain this in more detail. We see this same principle in the next verse of Deuteronomy 6.

Deuteronomy 6:3

Hear therefore, O Israel, and be careful to do them (commandment = Lord), that it may go well with you (blessing = Savior), and that you may multiply greatly, as the Lord, the God of your fathers, has promised you, in a land flowing with milk and honey (blessing = Savior).

> Note in the above verses:
> The blessing from God being *Savior* comes AFTER one meets the condition of submitting to Him as *Lord*.

I wish everyone reading this would take a couple minutes to just let the preceding sentence sink in. That doesn't mean we have to be perfect, but it does mean God's blessings are generally for those who trust Him and are walking with Him. The rest of this book unpacks this critical biblical principle.

The nature of God is such that He rules over all of creation and creatures so as to protect and bless them. In order to do this, God issues commandments that He expects us to obey. These commandments are not haphazard or arbitrary, but for our own good.

Deuteronomy 6:24

*And the Lord commanded us to do all these statutes, to fear the Lord our God (Lord), **for our good always**, that he might preserve us alive, as we are this day (Savior).*

163

The New Living Translation renders it this way:

*And the Lord our God commanded us to obey all these decrees and to fear him **so he can continue to bless us** and preserve our lives, as he has done to this day.*

He issues commands for our own good, to bless us. What's behind this is the fact that He knows more than we do—infinitely more. This is theology 101...God knows everything and we don't.

Does the parent of a ten-year-old boy tell him not to play video games all day long because they don't want their son to have fun? No, it's because playing video games all day long is harmful to their son and would prevent him from other academic, recreational and social activities that would result in a more balanced, well-rounded and grounded teenager and young adult. The parent knows more than the child, so these instructions are issued from the foundation of experience, knowledge and wisdom. The command was given for their own good.

Deuteronomy 10:12-13

*And now, Israel, what does the Lord your God require of you, but to fear the Lord your God, to walk in all his ways, to love him, to serve the Lord your God with all your heart and with all your soul, and to keep the commandments and statutes of the Lord, which I am commanding you today (Lord) **for your good** (Savior)?*

God's nature is to bless, but in doing so He must issue commandments because He, in His wisdom, knows what is best for us. Issuing commandments is tied to His nature as *Lord*. The subsequent blessings He bestows are tied to His nature as *Savior*. So these are the titles of Jesus' two-fold nature.

Acts 2:36

*Let all the house of Israel therefore know for certain that God has made him **both Lord and Christ**, this Jesus whom you crucified."*

Notice the titles, *Lord* and *Christ* (Messiah, Deliverer, One who saves). Let's look at these titles in more detail.

Chapter 17

A Savior to be Received From

I am eternally grateful that I serve a Savior who saved me from my sins and granted me eternal life. I needed a Savior because I was "dead in trespasses and sins" (Ephesians 2:1). I was born with the sin nature and had no release from it until I accepted Christ at the age of seventeen. Words cannot express my gratitude for Jesus Christ, the Savior, paying the price for my sin on the cross.

Colossians 2:13-14

You were dead because of your sins and because your sinful nature was not yet cut away. Then God made you alive with Christ, for he forgave all our sins. He canceled the record of the charges against us and took it away by nailing it to the cross.

Jesus' mission as Savior and Deliverer was declared from His birth.

Matthew 1:21

*She will bear a son, and you shall call his name Jesus, for he will **save his people from their sins**.*

Luke 2:11

*For unto you is born this day in the city of David **a Savior, who is Christ the Lord**.*

In the most general sense, a "savior" is one who saves or delivers. The Merriam-Webster Online Dictionary states that the word *savior* means, *one that saves from danger or destruction*[18] (hence, the life ring on *Savior* on the book cover). We might even use the term in a secular sense, such as when someone has a flat tire at night in the middle of nowhere. They might exclaim, "In the middle of my frightening predicament, when I didn't know what to do and where there was no cell phone coverage, up drives a *savior*, parked his car behind me, got out and changed my tire in ten minutes. As it turns out, he was a car mechanic." I've seen magazine or newspaper articles using the word *savior* for someone who turned a company around.

In Matthew 1:21 above (*shall His name Jesus, for He will save His people from their sins*), there is a connection between the name "Jesus" and the title Savior, "for he will save his people from their sins." What is this connection? It's because the name "Jesus" is the Greek form of the Hebrew name we know as "Joshua." The Hebrew **transliteration** (the process of converting non-western alphabetical characters, in this case Hebrew, into western characters we recognize) is *Yĕhowshuwa*, the **translation** being "Jehovah is Salvation." So intrinsic to the name "Jesus" is that He will save, as in, "save his people from their sins."

Now we come to the title "Savior" itself. The title is used in both the Old and New Testaments.

2 Samuel 22:3

*My God, my rock, in whom I take refuge, my shield, and the horn of my **salvation**, my stronghold and my refuge, my **savior**; you **save** me from violence.*

Notice the connection between *savior, salvation* and *save*. The Hebrew word (the Old Testament was written in Hebrew) for "Savior" is *yasha'* and means, "save, savior, deliver, help, helper, defend, avenge, and rescue." It's always connected to the act of saving, rescuing and delivering.

2 Kings 13:5

*Therefore the LORD gave Israel a **savior**, so that they **escaped from the hand of** the Syrians, and the people of Israel lived in their homes as formerly.*

---

[18] https://www.merriam-webster.com/dictionary/savior

Again, we see the connection between "savior" and delivering, saving and rescuing people. And, of course, this is when we cry out for a Savior.

Jeremiah 14:8

*O you hope of Israel, its **savior** in time of trouble.*

We are so thankful for a Savior in times of trouble. He is "a very present help in trouble" (Psalm 46:1). God wants us to call upon Him in times of trouble.

Hebrews 4:16

Let us then with confidence draw near to the throne of grace, that we may receive mercy and find grace to help in time of need.

When we come to the New Testament, the title "Savior" refers to Jesus Christ.

Luke 2:11

*For unto you is born this day in the city of David a **Savior**, who is Christ the Lord.*

John 4:42

*They said to the woman, "It is no longer because of what you said that we believe, for we have heard for ourselves, and we know that this is indeed the **Savior** of the world."*

1 John 4:14

*And we have seen and testify that the Father has sent his Son to be the **Savior** of the world.*

In the New Testament, the title "Savior" is the Greek word *sōtēr.* It means, "deliverer, preserver, protector, one who saves." All of God's blessings bestowed upon us through Christ issue forth from His being our *Savior.*

Titus 3:4-6

> *But when the **goodness and loving kindness** of God our **Savior** appeared, he **saved us**, not because of works done by us in righteousness, but according to his own mercy, by the washing of regeneration and renewal of the Holy Spirit, whom he **poured out on us** richly **through Jesus Christ our Savior.***

All of God's richest blessings come to us "through Jesus Christ our Savior." This title *Savior, **sōtēr**,* comes from its Greek root word, ***sōzō,*** which means, "to save, deliver, protect, heal and make whole." One is the noun (Savior), one is the verb (save). For example, it's used three times in Matthew 9:20-22.

Matthew 9:20-22

> *And behold, a woman who had suffered from a discharge of blood for twelve years came up behind him and touched the fringe of his garment, for she said to herself, "If I only touch his garment, I will be **made well** (sōzō)." Jesus turned, and seeing her he said, "Take heart, daughter; your faith has **made you well** (sōzō)." And instantly the woman was **made well** (sōzō).*

You can't separate the *title* from the *actions* the title performs. The Savior saves. The Healer heals. The Deliverer delivers. The Protector protects. One is the title of Christ and the other is the action He takes. He is indeed a Savior to be received from.

What qualifies Jesus as Savior is because He wasn't stained with sin or the sin nature when He was born in Bethlehem. All born from the seed of man (you and I), are born slaves to sin.

Romans 5:12

> *Therefore, just as sin came into the world through one man, and death through sin, and so **death spread to all men** because all sinned.*

All descendants of Adam had death and sin infect them from birth. We were all born into the slave market of sin. And the principle is: slaves can't free slaves, only free men can free slaves. So God, from the very beginning, had a plan for Adam and Eve's sin. The first prophecy about a coming Messiah comes the moment after the fall of man, being seduced by Satan. In talking to the devil, here's what God prophesied about his future demise.

Genesis 3:15

And I will put enmity (hostility) between you and the woman, and between your offspring and hers; he will crush your head, and you will strike his heel. (NIV)

This is the first prophecy about a coming Messiah who would crush Satan. There are three important points here.

1. There's coming a Messiah, a Deliverer to remedy things.
2. This offspring would be said to be the offspring of a woman, not a man. The foretells something.
3. Though Satan will strike the Messiah on his heel, He, the Messiah, would crush Satan's head.

The prophecy specifically mentions that the Messiah would be the offspring (seed – NASB) of a woman. Biblically, genealogies are always through the man, but here the Messiah will be born of a woman, no man mentioned. Why? The answer is—because this foretells a future virgin birth, no man involved!

Isaiah 7:14

*Therefore the Lord himself will give you a sign. Behold, **the virgin shall conceive and bear a son**, and shall call his name Immanuel.*

Galatians 4:4

*But when the fullness of time had come, God sent forth his Son, **born of woman**.*

Why would it say, "born of a woman," when everybody born here on Planet Earth is born of a woman? Because it indicates no man involved...a virgin birth. The reason the Savior had to be born of a virgin is because if born from the seed of a man, he would be born into the slave market of sin. But Jesus, being born of a woman without the Adamic stain of sin, was a free man, and only a free man can free a slave (you and me).

The prophecy also says that the devil will strike the Messiah on the heel but that the Messiah would crush Satan's head. If you were shot in the heel, it would be temporary, it would hurt, but you'd recover. But if you were shot in the head, that's fatal. Satan would have an initial victory in seeing Jesus Christ crucified. But it was temporary. Three days later, Christ crushed Satan's head, issuing him a fatal blow.

Colossians 2:14-15

Canceling the record of debt that stood against us with its legal demands. This he set aside, nailing it to the cross. **He disarmed the rulers and authorities and put them to open shame, by triumphing over them in him.**

Jesus dealt Satan a fatal crushing blow, fulfilling the Genesis 3:15 prophecy. A free man, freed from sin and the sin nature, paid the price for our sin on the cross; then rose victorious over sin, the grave, Satan and his kingdom. Jesus, the Savior, did all of this for us, and we are grateful.

This Savior of ours is not just a man who died on the cross. He is all God and all man at the same time. Through Paul's letters he alternately uses the phrase "God our Savior" and "Jesus Christ our Savior," indicating that He is both.

1 Timothy 2:3 – "God our Savior."
2 Timothy 1:10 – "Our Savior Christ Jesus."
Titus 3:4 – "God our Savior."
Titus 3:6 – "Jesus Christ our Savior."

There is one time Paul leaves no doubt about the message that Christ is both God and Savior.

Titus 2:13

Waiting for our blessed hope, the appearing of the glory of **our great God and Savior Jesus Christ.**

As stated earlier, all the blessings of salvation (eternal life), answered prayer, healing, provision, protection, and deliverance come from Jesus Christ being our Savior. We need a Savior because we need saving from our sin and its penalty, eternal death. When a person becomes born again, they believe on and receive Jesus Christ as their Savior and trust Him for their salvation and deliverance from sin and its consequences.

What I find interesting is that nowhere in the Bible does it talk about accepting Jesus Christ as Savior. We do and should of course, but accepting Christ as Savior isn't mentioned as primary. Scripture teaches accepting Jesus Christ as the other title, *Lord*.

Chapter 18

A Lord to be Obeyed

The two-fold nature of Jesus Christ is Lord and Savior. As Savior, He saved us from our sins (Matthew 1:21 – *She will bear a son, and you shall call his name Jesus, **for he will save his people from their sins**.*). One reason we have been saved from our sins is so our relationship with God can be restored, and consequently experience eternal life. But just like the title "Savior" is linked to who Christ is and what He did (does), He possesses another title, "Lord," which also links to who He is and what He does. This title "Lord" implies one to serve and obey. The reason we have been set free from sin as a result of Christ's work on the cross as Savior, is to now be free to serve God in holiness. We've been freed from sin (Savior) in order to obey and serve God (Lord).

Romans 6:17-19, 22

> *But thanks be to God, that you who were **once slaves of sin have become obedient from the heart** to the standard of teaching to which you were committed, and, **having been set free from sin, have become slaves of righteousness**. I am speaking in human terms, because of your natural limitations. For just as you **once presented your members as slaves to impurity and to lawlessness** leading to more lawlessness, so **now present your members as slaves to righteousness leading to sanctification**. ... But now that you have been **set free from sin** and have become **slaves of God**, the **fruit you get leads to sanctification and its end, eternal life**.*

Notice the connection between these elements:

Set free from sin → Slaves to God → Fruit in the form of sanctification → Eternal life.

If it's a true salvation (by grace through faith), it will result in servanthood and obedience to God, which will produce fruit—this true salvation resulting in eternal life.

Romans 6 states that we've been set free from sin so that we can now serve God and walk in holiness. Failing to understand this point is failing to comprehend the full purpose and nature of salvation. This takes us to the other title or office that Jesus Christ stands in, that of *Lord*. Not understanding this has led many people to experience what was talked about previously, a false conversion, or a salvation forfeited.

Matthew 7:21-23

> Not everyone who **says** to me, "**Lord, Lord,**" will enter the kingdom of heaven, but the one who does the will of my Father who is in heaven. On that day many will say to me, "Lord, Lord, did we not prophesy in your name, and cast out demons in your name, and do many mighty works in your name?" And then will I declare to them, "I never knew you; depart from me, you **workers of lawlessness.**"

Titus 1:16

> They **profess** to know God, but they deny him by their works.

According to Romans 6, the purpose for being set free from sin (a result of Savior) is so that we no longer serve lawlessness, but serve God (honoring Him as Lord). Here in Matthew 7, many people believed in Jesus as Savior but continued in their lawlessness. There was a disconnect in their lives between Jesus as *Savior* and Jesus as *Lord*. That disconnect cost them their eternity.

The title "Lord" in the New Testament is the Greek word *Kurios*. It means:

- Lord
- Master
- He to whom a person belongs, about which he has power of deciding (Thayer's Greek Lexicon)
- Supreme in authority

174

- Owner, one who has control of the person (Thayer's Greek Lexicon)
- Controller
- One to whom service is due on any ground (Vine's Expository Dictionary of N.T. Words)

It is from this title and office that God, through Jesus Christ, issues commands. He can issue commands because He is Lord, Master, supreme in authority (hence the crown on "Lord" on the book cover). He can issue commands because He is Controller. He can issue commands because we belong to Him (1 Corinthians 6:20 – *we've been bought with a price*) and therefore He has the power of deciding over us. If Jesus is our Lord, He can expect service from us *on any ground* (for any reason and under any condition).

I don't think it's a stretch to say that the people in Matthew 7:21-23 didn't "accept" or honor Jesus as Lord (although they called Him that), only as Savior, intellectually acknowledging who He was but not submitted to His reign in their lives. Consequently, Jesus said to them, "I never knew you." This leads us to an unfortunate reality.

> It's possible to accept Jesus as Savior but not as Lord.

But I submit to you that, to be saved, we must receive and honor Jesus Christ as both Lord and Savior.

Does the Bible give us any clues on what being born again means, as it relates to these terms...Lord and Savior? The answer is yes. And notice which title is connected to the salvation experience.

Romans 10:9,10

*If you confess with your mouth that **Jesus is Lord** and believe in your heart that God raised him from the dead, **you will be saved**. For with the heart one believes and is justified, and with the mouth one confesses and is **saved**.*

The word "saved," is the Greek word *sōzō*, and is where we get the title "Savior" (*sōtēr*) from. Being "saved" is a result of Jesus being our *Savior*, as discussed earlier. But...being saved is a result of the first part of the verse, confessing, accepting and honoring

Jesus as **Lord**! In other words, when we repent, believe, receive and commit to follow Jesus Christ as **Lord**, the One who is supreme in authority in our lives, we experience salvation that issues forth from Christ being our **Savior**. This is the reverse of the people in Matthew 7:21-23, who accepted Jesus as *Savior* but not *Lord*.

- Receiving Christ as Savior but not Lord = eternal destruction.

- Receiving Christ as Lord and Savior = eternal life

It's believing and calling upon Jesus as Lord that is connected to salvation. Of course we also receive Him as Savior at the same time, but I find it interesting and important that being saved is connected to acknowledging Christ as Lord, *Kurios*, supreme in authority. We see this principle in other places as well.

Romans 10:13

*For "everyone who calls on the name of the **Lord** will be **saved**."*

Call upon Him as *Kurios* (Lord) and you will be *sōzō* (saved).

Acts 16:31

*And they said, "Believe in the **Lord** Jesus, and you will be **saved**, you and your household."*

Here we see the very same connection between believing (surrendering, following and trusting in) Jesus as **Lord** with the resulting **salvation**, salvation accomplished from Christ being our Savior. The born-again experience is based upon receiving Christ as Lord, Master, Supreme in Authority, Owner and Controller. If we're not **willing** (a matter of intention) to receive and follow Him as Lord, we're not saved. That's the whole essence of Luke 14:25ff—becoming a disciple of Christ by loving everyone and everything else in life LESS THAN our love for Jesus, counting the cost, denying ourselves, picking up our cross and following Him. It is about surrendering to His Lordship and allowing Him to reign as Supreme in Authority in our lives that results in salvation. It's forsaking all and everything to follow Christ.

Mark 10:29-30

*Truly, I say to you, there is no one who has **left** house or brothers or sisters or mother or father or children or lands, for my sake and for the gospel, who will not receive a hundredfold now in this time, houses and brothers and sisters and mothers and children and lands, with persecutions, and in the age to come eternal life.*

It's about leaving, forsaking all and everything for the sake of Jesus Christ. It results in eternal life. Not forsaking all and everything puts that in peril.

When I was pastoring in Rochester, New York, in the mid-1980s, we took teams of two into neighborhoods to go witnessing house-to-house. It really didn't work then and doesn't work now, but that's a different story. My partner and I went to one house, and the door was answered by a young man who was around twenty years old. We engaged him in a good discussion and after sharing with him the "Good News" about receiving Christ and gaining eternal life, he was agreeable to pray "the sinner's prayer" with us. After leading him through that prayer, we instructed him on his next steps to walk in his new faith in Christ; read the Bible to get to know God, pray in this new relationship with Christ, learn to worship Christ, and attend church so that he can learn and fellowship from other believers. Right after we said that this young man said, "I'm not doing any of that." I was shocked to say the least. Without batting an eye, he said, "Well, I want Jesus and eternal life, but I'm not doing those other things."

The problem was that this young man was perfectly agreeable to receive Jesus as *Savior*, but had no desire or intention of surrendering Him as *Lord*. Actually, the problem was caused by our leaving out critical elements of what it truly means to accept Christ and be born again. It was our fault, not his. It's like me with the Publishing Clearing House entry to get $5,000 for life. The only thing I have to do is submit my name and information and my entry is in? Sure, so I fill it out. It's only later I find out I have to keep filling out a myriad of other surveys and checklists before I get something in the mail that says I'm a "finalist," and even then, they want to lick stamps on a form and send it in! If I would have known that I would have said no to the whole transaction. It was the same kind of thing with this young man.

We didn't share with him the full story of what was expected (the FULL gospel). We didn't talk about the need to repent of his sins, we didn't explain the cost of becoming a disciple of Jesus Christ, we didn't explain Jesus as *Lord*, only as *Savior*. But in its essence, getting "saved," as we saw from Romans 10, is directly connected to confessing and trusting in Jesus Christ as *Lord*. It is agreeing to step down from the throne of our lives and allowing Jesus to sit on that throne, allowing Him to call the shots, and surrender to His Lordship or rulership. Everyone has a throne in their life, and there is someone or something on that throne, whatever is most important in your life. With some people their kids sit on the throne. With some people their career is on the throne. Still others may have sports, adventure and partying on the throne. With some it's spending and shopping. If we are not willing to step down from the throne of our lives and instill Jesus upon that throne, we have missed the whole point of receiving Him.

In Luke 19, Jesus taught a parable about a nobleman going to another country to receive a kingdom and be crowned king. There was a problem however.

Luke 19:14

*But his citizens hated him and sent a delegation after him, saying, '**We do not want this man to reign over us.**'*

Long story short, at the end of the parable, here's what the nobleman said to those unwilling to accept his reign and crown him as king:

Luke 19:27

*But as for these enemies of mine, **who did not want me to reign over them**, bring them here and slaughter them before me.'"*

This is a parable about Jesus leaving Heaven, coming to earth and initiating a new Kingdom over which He would reign as "King of kings and Lord of lords" (Revelation 19:16). The crux of the issue was the citizens' acceptance or rejection of His reign over their lives. The ones who didn't want the king to reign over them are called *enemies* and summarily received a severe judgment and sentence. The essence of being born again is instilling Christ as King over our lives, and being willing to submit to His reign and rulership. Principle:

> We believe, accept and surrender to Jesus as **Lord**, resulting in receiving salvation from Him as being **Savior**.

But first thing is first, bowing to Him as Lord. The results of salvation follow. We see this order (Lord then Savior) with Christ's titles in 2 Peter.

2 Peter 1:11

*For in this way there will be richly provided for you an entrance into the eternal kingdom of our **Lord and Savior** Jesus Christ.*

2 Peter 2:20

*For if, after they have escaped the defilements of the world through the knowledge of our **Lord and Savior** Jesus Christ, they are again entangled in them and overcome, the last state has become worse for them than the first.*

2 Peter 3:1-2

*I am stirring up your sincere mind by way of reminder, that you should remember the predictions of the holy prophets and the commandment of the **Lord and Savior** through your apostles*

2 Peter 3:18

*But grow in the grace and knowledge of our **Lord and Savior** Jesus Christ.*

I believe the order to be deliberate: Lord, then Savior. This is why so few people who respond to altar calls or say "the sinner's prayer" follow through and become ongoing disciples of Jesus Christ. They, for the most part, accept Christ as Savior but have no intention of acknowledging Him as Lord, a Lord to be followed and obeyed.

Remember earlier that the two titles, Lord and Savior, mean two different things with different expressions or manifestations. "Lord" means supreme in authority, controller, master, owner, decider; whereas "Savior" means "deliverer, one who saves, healer, protector and sustainer." When we see God issuing commands, it comes from His nature as Lord; and when we see Him blessing, saving, answering prayer, healing, protecting and sustaining (providing), it comes from His nature as Savior. But here is the essential proposition of this whole book:

> He's not just a **Savior** to be received from, He's a **Lord** to be obeyed.

Accepting Christ on terms short of this is deficient. Not allowing the King to reign over us has ramifications. But Christ is both Lord and Savior, and Lord speaks of rulership.

Acts 5:31

> *God exalted him at his right hand as **Leader** (Prince – NIV) and **Savior**, to give repentance to Israel and forgiveness of sins.*

Leader or Prince speaks of His kingdom reign. Christ is both Leader and Savior. But most altar calls only focus on taking Him as Savior in order to experience eternal life. But, like Thomas, we must fall on our faces before Christ and acknowledge who He truly is.

John 20:28

> *Thomas answered him, "My Lord and my God!"*

There is something grossly deficient about willing to receive Him as Savior to gain eternal life, but having no intention or willingness to submit to Him as Lord.

LORDSHIP SALVATION

Now we come to a point of clarification, because I will undoubtedly be labeled as promoting something called, *Lordship Salvation*, but that depends on its definition.

I received Christ in June 1970 at the age of seventeen. At the time of this writing I am sixty-four years old. That's kind of old. My grandkids think I read the Old Testament just to reminisce. So, for forty-seven years I've had both feet in evangelical Christianity. Every now and then I'll hear or see this pithy little saying:

If He's not Lord of all—He's not Lord at all.

It sounds right, and although I believe in the nugget of truth expressed there, I technically don't believe it. Which one of us has every single area of our lives 100% submitted to the Lordship of Jesus Christ, meaning, every area of our life is godly and Christ-ruled?

The Apostle Paul prayed an interesting prayer for the Ephesians disciples. Keep in mind, the people Paul was writing to were already "saved." His prayer for them was:

Ephesians 3:16-17

*To be strengthened with power through his Spirit in your inner being, so **that Christ may dwell in your hearts through faith**.*

Get a hold of this...Paul is praying that Christ may dwell in their hearts even though Christ ALREADY resided in their hearts through faith! So what is Paul driving at here?

The verb "dwell" is in the present tense. Paul, even though these Ephesians disciples had already accepted Christ in the past, is praying that Christ will CONTINUE to dwell in their hearts through faith. The term "heart" means the very core of our desires and affections. And the truth is, we have many rooms in our heart that need to be submitted to the Lordship of Jesus Christ. Does Jesus dwell and have Lordship over the room in our heart with the sign over the door that says "Finances and Giving?" Does Jesus have full control over the room called "Spare Time and Recreation?" Does Jesus dwell in rule in the room called "Romance and Sex?" Does Jesus rule in the room called "Church Attendance and Volunteerism?"

If we define *Lordship Salvation* as claiming believers must have every area of their life fully submitted to the Lordship of Christ and the will of God or they're not saved, then *Lordship Salvation* is error. However, I don't believe expecting and teaching true believers to progressively yield to the control of Jesus as Lord over every room in their heart is *Lordship Salvation*. I believe that to be biblical discipleship.

Chapter 19

Son or Servant?

I come out of a theological tradition that majors on our *sonship* in Christ. "Sonship" means the relationship between the father and his sons (or generically, children) and is linked to rights of inheritance.

Ephesians 1:3-6

Blessed be the God and Father of our Lord Jesus Christ, who has blessed us in Christ with every spiritual blessing in the heavenly places, even as he chose us in him before the foundation of the world, that we should be holy and blameless before him. In love ***he predestined us for adoption to himself as sons through Jesus Christ.***

Romans 8:17

If children, then heirs—heirs of God and fellow ***heirs with Christ.***

In this tradition, there is a great deal of focus on being sons and daughters of God and therefore heirs with an inheritance. This inheritance includes all the blessings we have in Christ, which are many.

At the time of this writing, I am working full-time at an elder law office which specializes in wills, trusts, powers of attorney, guardianships, conservatorships and long-term care planning. I can assure you that the subject of inheritance can be quite exciting if on the receiving end of one. And so it is with Christians. When you teach on our inheritance in Christ, people love it.

Colossians 3:24

Knowing that from the Lord you will receive the inheritance as your reward.

If you want some regular and robust "amens" during a sermon, just preach about healing, provision, victory, overcoming, success, overcoming faith, our authority over the devil, and our inheritance. A good foundational verse for sonship would be Galatians 4:7.

Galatians 4:7

*So you are **no longer a slave, but a son**, and if a son, then an heir through God.*

That's exciting, and I would have to add, it's all true. I agree with it. I love it. But it's not the full story because then we come to Romans 6:22 and God rains on our parade.

Romans 6:22

*But now that you have been set free from sin and **have become slaves of God**, the fruit you get leads to sanctification and its end, eternal life.*

Oh boy, now we have an apparent contradiction:

"Have become slaves of God" (Romans 6:22)
"No longer a slave" (Galatians 4:7)

What are we to make of this? Are we sons or slaves, which is it? The answer is, both. Let me explain.

To understand Galatians 4:7 (*no longer a slave, but a son*), we must look at the context surrounding it. Galatians 3 and 4 is talking about slavery to the law, not servanthood to God. The Apostle Paul is teaching here that believers in Christ are no longer slaves to the Mosaic law. In Greek culture, a young boy was not part of the family, but instead was brought up by a slave-tutor and was treated as a slave himself. At the age of fourteen or fifteen, the boy went through a ceremony called the Toga Virilis, cloak of manhood, and was adopted into his own family as a son with full rights. Paul is teaching that the Mosaic law was our slave-tutor that eventually led us to Christ, and now we have been adopted into God's family as full heirs with Christ. In relationship to the Old Testament law, we are no longer under it's control or tutelage, but now adopted in as sons and heirs.

To interpret Galatians 4:7 as saying we are not slaves or servants of God anymore is to completely misinterpret the verse. The fact is...we are slaves or the more commonly used word, servants of Christ. Romans 6:22 says that we have been freed from sin and now *slaves* of God. And slaves obey their master! Woe to Christians who don't understand that we are slaves to God and that Jesus Christ is our Lord and Master. Jesus Christ is a Lord to be obeyed!

Some quote John 15:15 in protest.

John 15:15

No longer do I call you servants, for the servant does not know what his master is doing; but I have called you friends, for all that I have heard from my Father I have made known to you.

But we must keep in mind that this was from the perspective of Jesus to His disciples whom He had travelled with 24/7 for three years. Servants aren't filled in with knowledge, they're just told what to do. Jesus is making the point that as Jesus' friends, He makes known to them intimate knowledge of the Father. But this does not negate that our perspective upward toward Jesus is that we are, yes, friends, but servants as well. And servants do that they are commanded. In fact, just look at the previous verse.

John 15:14

You are my friends (if you do what I command you.

Jesus even connects the nature of friendship with Him to obedience to His commands!

If we focus only on *sons not slaves*, we lose sight of the other aspect of our relationship with the Lord. Romans 12:3 exhorts us not to think more highly of ourselves than we ought to think, but this is exactly what happens with people who are *sons not slaves* focused.

There are a number of words for *slave* in Greek in the New Testament. One is a slave taken in war, another is one born into slavery, and still another is one who has enlisted to be a slave under someone of their own free will. When we were born again, we willingly became slaves to our new Master, Jesus Christ and are to obey Him.

Romans 6:19

> *For just as you once presented your members as **slaves** to impurity and to lawlessness leading to more lawlessness, so now present your members as **slaves** to righteousness leading to sanctification.*

We used to be slaves of impurity and lawlessness, but now we are slaves to righteousness. The overriding principle here is found in 2 Peter 19.

2 Peter 2:19

> *For whatever overcomes a person, to that he is enslaved.*

Because I am born again, I have been overcome with love and adoration for Christ, and therefore to Him I have become enslaved. If we lose sight of this relationship to Christ we lose accountability to Him, and that leads to drifting into sin or lukewarmness. Romans 6:19 says that when we present our bodies as slaves to righteousness, it leads to sanctification, which is the progressive process of holiness. And three verses later, Romans 6:22, we find the end of being slaves to God...sanctification:

> *But now that you have been set free from sin and have become **slaves of God**, the fruit you get leads to **sanctification** and its end, **eternal life**.*

Slaves to God → Sanctification → Eternal Life

The danger is if we live life in either ditch, a *son only* or *slave only* mindset. We need to have both understandings, that we are sons and heirs, but also that we are slaves to Christ and righteousness. People who are *son only* minded relate mainly to Jesus as Savior. People who are *slave only* minded relate mainly to Christ as Lord. But He is both Lord and Savior, so we need balance as son and slave.

The believers in the early church certainly understood their relationship to the Lord.

Acts 4:29

*And now, **Lord**, look upon their threats and grant to your*
***servants** to continue to speak your word with all boldness.*

They addressed Him as "Lord" and looked upon themselves
as servants/slaves. Notices that connection between "Lord" and
viewing themselves as "servants." This must not be overlooked.

One aspect of the definition of slave is, "One who gives
himself up wholly to another's will. Devoted to another to the
disregard of one's own interests."[19] If we have accepted Jesus
Christ into our lives as Lord, not just Savior, we should ask
ourselves, "Is my will swallowed up in the will of Christ? Do I
subordinate my desires to His desires?" Doing so is being servant-
minded. Do I determine what I want to do, or do I make decisions
based on the will of my Master?

James 4:13-15

13 *Come now, you who say, "Today or tomorrow we will go into*
such and such a town and spend a year there and trade and
make a profit"—

14 *yet you do not know what tomorrow will bring. What is your*
life? For you are a mist that appears for a little time and
then vanishes.

15 *Instead you ought to say, "If the Lord wills, we will live and*
do this or that."

Servants of God pray and seek the mind of God on major
decisions.

As servants, we become devoted to the interests of our
Master and disregard our own. In truth, slaves do not have
choices! Slaves obey. The test in all of this is when the Holy Spirit
prompts us to act in a certain way. Will we ignore or will we obey?
When a missionary is speaking at church and it's time for the
offering to bless him or her, and we internally sense the Holy

---

19 https://www.blueletterbible.org/lang/lexicon/lexi-
con.cfm?Strongs=G1401&t=KJV

Spirit's nudging, "Write out a check for $300.00 to them," is our will swallowed up at that point in the will of our Master? Do we obey? When the Holy Spirit prompts us to ask someone about their eternal destiny, do we obey or stay quiet...playing it safe?

The Apostle Paul had a balanced sense of who he was and how he related to Christ. Notice Romans 1:1.

Romans 1:1

*Paul, a **servant** of Christ Jesus, called to be an **apostle**.*

The Holman Christian Standard Bible reads this way:

*Paul, a **slave** of Christ Jesus, called as an **apostle**.*

Notice what Paul listed first and then second: servant or slave, then apostle. His primary concern was to view himself as a servant or slave of Christ Jesus. Out of that primary relationship came his call as an apostle. I get amused these days, amused or annoyed, by how many pastors, teachers and evangelists refer to themselves for advertisement or when they've authored a book or magazine article. They're all *Bishops* or *Doctors*. Many of them do not have earned doctorates at all, they are honorary doctorates presented to them by a buddy in ministry who themselves don't have earned doctorates. Here's what I'd like to hear from them, "I'm a slave of Christ Jesus." But you'll never see that on an advertisement for a ministers' conference.

Going back to the objection raised regarding John 15:15:

John 15:15

No longer do I call you servants, for the servant does not know what his master is doing; but I have called you friends, for all that I have heard from my Father I have made known to you.

Does this verse contradict Romans 6:22: "You have been set free from sin and have become slaves of God?" No, it doesn't contradict it at all. First of all, in John 15:15 Jesus didn't say we weren't slaves. What He said was that He would no longer CALL us slaves. There's a difference. This verse is taken from Jesus' standpoint on how He perceives us, not on how we're to look at ourselves. Secondly, Jesus was trying to teach them their position in Him, in Christ. His disciples were used to three years of being viewed, more or less, as a slave.

Matthew 10:24-25

A disciple is not above his teacher, nor a servant above his master. It is enough for the disciple to be like his teacher, and the servant like his master. If they have called the master of the house Beelzebul, how much more will they malign those of his household.

Here Jesus clearly indicates Himself as the Master and His disciples as the servants (NLT uses the word *slaves*), and rightly so.

John 13:16

Truly, truly, I say to you, a servant is not greater than his master, nor is a messenger greater than the one who sent him.

Jesus was instructing His disciples in Luke 17 about servants.

Luke 17:7-10

7   *Will any one of you who has a servant plowing or keeping sheep say to him when he has come in from the field, "Come at once and recline at table"?*

8   *Will he not rather say to him, "Prepare supper for me, and dress properly, and serve me while I eat and drink, and afterward you will eat and drink"?*

9   *Does he thank the servant because he did what was commanded?*

10   *So you also, when you have done all that you were commanded, say, "We are unworthy servants; we have only done what was our duty."*

Wow! Can we grasp what Jesus is saying here? After obeying the Master we're not to puff out our chest and say, "What a good boy am I!" We're to understand that we are slaves, unworthy slaves at that. Yes, Christ made us worthy, but in and of ourselves, we are fundamentally unworthy.

In Luke 12:35-48, Jesus again likens His disciples to slaves. In Matthew 22:1-14, His disciples are likened to slaves. In Matthew 24:45-51, Jesus is looking for faithful and sensible slaves. So you see, the disciples, having travelled with Jesus night and day for three years, were used to hearing all this about being slaves, and Jesus now wanted to bring a new paradigm to their thinking about another complementary way of viewing their relationship...as friends! Therefore, we must interpret John 15:15 in this light. Jesus' view of His disciples is that they are both servants and friends, all at the same time because they complement each other, providing a balanced view of who we are to Him. John 15:15 doesn't negate the principle that we are His servants, it just adds another dimension to the relationship.

The fact is, we are slaves of Christ Jesus.

Romans 6:16

*Do you not know that if you present yourselves to anyone as **obedient slaves, you are slaves of the one whom you obey**, either of sin, which leads to death, or of obedience, which leads to righteousness?*

You are a slave to the one you obey. Period. That sounds like what we read earlier in 2 Peter 2:19, "For you are a slave to whatever controls you." (NLT) The Lord wants us to have a servant mentality. We see this in Philippians 2.

Philippians 2:3-8

3   *Do nothing from selfish ambition or conceit, but in humility count others more significant than yourselves.*

4   *Let each of you look not only to his own interests, but also to the interests of others.*

5   ***Have this mind among yourselves**, which is yours in Christ Jesus,*

6   *who, though he was in the form of God, did not count equality with God a thing to be grasped,*

7   *but emptied himself, by **taking the form of a servant**, being born in the likeness of men.*

8   *And being found in human form, he humbled himself by **becoming obedient** to the point of death, even death on a cross.*

Have this mind, acquire this mentality—humble yourself, take the form of a servant and become obedient. Focusing in on our inheritance and rights is more connected to a *son* mentality, tapping into the promises that come from Christ as Savior. Focusing in on obeying and serving is more connected to a *servant* mentality, staying keenly aware that we are slaves.

1 Corinthians 7:22

For the one who was a slave when called to faith in the Lord is the Lord's freed person; similarly, the one who was free when called is Christ's slave. (NIV)

Actual slaves who accepted Christ could rejoice because in Christ, they are free. Those not slaves when accepting Christ are called "Christ's slave." We are not slaves that cower in fear of the Master. We willingly offer ourselves fully as servants to the most loving and kind Master of all, Jesus Christ.

Chapter 20

Lord-Minded vs. Savior-Minded

Spiritual growth (discipleship) is marked by an increase awareness of Jesus Christ as Lord, Master, Owner—the One, as slaves of Christ, whom we obey and serve. We still, of course, relate to Jesus Christ as Savior by praying, asking and receiving by faith the promises afforded us "in Christ." We stay eternally grateful for escaping the wrath of God and look forward to eternal life in heaven. We aren't hesitant to pray for healing and provision. When in trouble, we run to our Savior with confidence.

Hebrews 4:16

Let us then with confidence draw near to the throne of grace, that we may receive mercy and find grace to help in time of need.

Yet, as we grow in Christ, our focus shifts more and more to loving and serving God through Jesus Christ. More and more our mindset shifts from being Savior-minded to Lord-minded, at least to the point of balance. What is the difference? Are there any telltale signs that differentiate these mindsets? This table may help.

	Savior-Minded	Lord-Minded
1.	Praise God for what He's done.	Praise God for who He is.
2.	I'm not longer a slave, I'm son with rights and an inheritance	I realize I'm a slave, my heart is set on obeying my Lord.
3.	I turn to God in times of trouble.	I turn to God daily and abide in Him continually.

4.	I want God's intervention, but not His interference in my life.	I want both God's intervention and His interference.
5.	I serve God on my terms.	I serve God on His terms.
6.	God serves me and answers all my prayers.	I serve God and His will.
7.	I need good reasons before I obey.	I obey without having to be told good reasons.
8.	I need to see the whole picture before I step out and obey.	I only need to obey one step at a time.
9.	I know God but don't honor Him as God. Romans 1:21	I know God and honor Him as God.
10.	I contemplate all my choices.	I understand that I'm a slave and don't have choices.
11.	I make decisions on what I think is best. I'll go where I want and do what I want.	I make decisions by first paying and asking God for wisdom and His will. James 4:13-15
12.	I look for a robe.	I look for a towel.
13.	I walk on the widest edge of the narrow road.	I walk on the centerline of the narrow road.
14.	My motive for obedience is reward.	My motive for obedience is love for my Master and Lord.
15.	I'm sorry for the consequences of sin.	I'm sorry for offending a holy God whom I love and serve.
16.	I was mad when they said unto me, "Let us go up to the house of the Lord today."	I was glad when they said unto me, "Let us go up to the house of the Lord today." Psalm 122:1
17.	I pray because I'm expected to.	I pray because I love talking to my heavenly Father.
18.	I read God's Word because of duty.	I read God's Word because I live on every word that proceeds out of the mouth of God.
19.	I'm assured salvation because I received Christ as Savior a number of years ago.	I'm assured salvation because I received Christ a number of years ago and I stay faithful to Him through worship and works of obedience.

The point of this is to guard oneself from being imbalanced on either side of the equation. Being Savior-focused only can lead to looseness in regards to walking faithfully with the Lord in obedience and holiness. Being Lord-minded only can lead to legalism and pride. We need to strike a balance because Christ is both Lord and Savior.

Chapter 21

The Fear of the Lord

2 Corinthians 5:11

*Therefore, **knowing the fear of the Lord**, we persuade others.*

This verse defines the problem...we do NOT know the fear of the Lord.

I believe "others" can be applied to both believer and unbeliever alike. If we know the fear of the Lord, we'll persuade unbelievers that God is real, salvation through Christ is offered, but a rejection of that offer results in eternal destruction. But in context, the verse is addressed to believers. The two verses before this, verses 9 and 10, talk about pleasing the Lord and the judgment seat of Christ to be judged by our, dare we say it, works!

2 Corinthians 5:9-10

9 *So whether we are at home or away, we make it our aim to please him.*

10 *For we must all appear before the judgment seat of Christ, so that each one may receive what is due for **what he has done** in the body, whether good or evil.*

In the context of believers being judged for their works, Paul goes on to say in verse 11, "Therefore, knowing the fear of the Lord, we persuade others."

Judged on what we've done has nothing to do with deeds aimed at earning God's favor in salvation. Salvation comes by grace alone through faith alone. Judged on what we've done is referring to works AFTER accepting Christ, what we've called faithfulness and works of obedience. So "knowing the fear of the Lord" as it concerns the judgment seat of Christ, "we persuade others." Yet, I'm not aware of much persuading going on toward other Christians regarding this upcoming judgment seat of Christ. When was the last time any of us had a conversation with another Christian, warning them about the judgment seat of Christ and their lukewarmness? Maybe it's because there's another kind of fear that outweighs our fear of the Lord...the fear of confrontation with other people.

Proverbs 29:25

The fear of man brings a snare. (NASB)

I repeat what I said starting off this chapter— we do NOT know the fear of the Lord. But the fear of the Lord must outweigh the fear of man.

Acts 4:19

Peter and John answered them, "Whether it is right in the sight of God to listen to you rather than to God, you must judge.

Acts 5:29

But Peter and the apostles answered, "We must obey God rather than men.

Fear of the Lord must be our priority. The reason most people don't possess a healthy, reverent fear of God is due to an imbalanced view of His nature. God created man in His own image (Genesis 1:26), but we have reversed it and have created God in our image! We project onto God our view of what He *ought* to be. And so to many, God is so all-loving and merciful that He would never judge or pronounce sentence on anyone. He's so loving that He would never impose a sentence of hell on anyone, thus leading to the heresy of *universalism* (everybody eventually goes to heaven). We love and embrace the view of God being our *Daddy*, our *Abba Father*, crawling up on His lap and having this love relationship with, and reject the view of God being "an all-consuming fire" (Hebrews 12:29). We opt for one side of God's nature at the expense of the other. But He has both.

Romans 11:22

*Behold then the **kindness and severity** of God; to those who fell, severity, but to you, God's kindness, **if** you continue in His kindness; otherwise you also will be cut off. (NASB)*

Here we see the two aspects of God's nature: kindness and severity, depending on how we respond to Him. It's interesting that "awful" and "awesome" come from the same root word. Whether it's awesome or awful depends. The two sides to God's character as expressed here in Romans 11 are kindness and severity. These two aspects of His nature issue forth out of His nature as Lord and Savior...severity and judgment connected to Him being Lord and kindness to deliver and rescue connected to Him being Savior. But, as always, humanity gravitates toward the one side of God's nature...the kindness. But we forget the other side of God's nature that is very real.

Colossians 3:5-8

5   *Put to death therefore what is earthly in you: sexual immorality, impurity, passion, evil desire, and covetousness, which is idolatry.*

6   *On account of these the wrath of God is coming.*

7   *In these you too once walked, when you were living in them.*

8   *But now you must put them all away.*

We forget that "the wrath of God is coming." Only by understanding the other side of God's nature, severity, do we acquire a healthy fear of the Lord. Even as believers, flirting with sin can and should be mitigated by a healthy fear of God.

Hebrews 10:26-27

*For **if we go on sinning deliberately** after receiving the knowledge of the truth, there no longer remains a sacrifice for sins, but **a fearful expectation of judgment**, and a fury of fire that will consume the adversaries.*

A fearful expectation of judgment can drastically reduce the practice of sin. This reverent and healthy fear of God does not negate understanding or receiving His love. We can both love God and fear Him at the same time. I loved my father, but I feared him at the same time. My dad had a certain tone of voice that struck fear in my heart—"Now listen here young man!" I can still hear in my head how that sounded. I loved my dad and he loved me, but I still maintained a healthy fear of him. But as believers, we have lost this healthy, reverent fear of God, and it has affected how we do life.

"When there is no fear of God, people have to invent a gospel of convenience." - David Wilkerson [20]

A healthy fear is always connected to a realization of accountability.

Matthew 12:36-37

I tell you, on the day of judgment people will **give account** *for every careless word they speak, for by your words you will be justified, and by your words you will be condemned.*

If I understand that I will be called to account, I maintain a healthy fear, which in turn leads to behavior aligned with uprightness. The opposite is true as well: If I believe there is no realistic accountability, I don't fear, and my behavior loosens up and naturally gravitates toward waywardness and sin. And that is the place, for the most part, the Body of Christ is at, at least in the western world. It has led to what is called "hyper-grace."

Hyper-grace theology is a big problem. It says that we're now under grace (which is true) and that sin is not a problem (which is not true). It says that when Jesus died for your sins, all your sins were in the future (which is obviously true), therefore all your sins have been paid for on the cross (which is true), and therefore all your sins have been forgiven (which is not true). Just because Jesus paid for our sins doesn't mean they are forgiven. The price has been paid, but we must still confess and repent of our sins.

1 John 1:9

---

[20]   https://worldchallenge.org/content/its-time-get-right-god

If we confess our sins, he is faithful and just to forgive us our sins and to cleanse us from all unrighteousness.

Forgiveness comes after confession and repentance. But hyper-grace teachers say we're forgiven for all sins, even future sins. But that's unscriptural.

2 Peter 1:9

*But whoever does not have them is nearsighted and blind, forgetting that they have been cleansed **from their past sins.** (NIV)*

Scripture teaches we've been cleansed from our **past** sins, not present and future sins. We're only cleansed of sins we commit presently when, according to 1 John 1:9, we confess them.

It is this hyper-grace teaching that has seeped into the western Body of Christ and caused untold damage. The verse cited earlier, 2 Corinthians 5:11, *Therefore, knowing the fear of the Lord, we persuade others*, is not a reality with them. They do not possess a healthy, reverent fear of God. This results in what is called an "easy-believism." This is defined as simply believe intellectually, and salvation is yours. And so, people believe that Jesus died and rose again much the same as they would believe we first walked on the moon in 1969. It's just believing intellectual facts with no commitment, no throwing themselves wholly into Christ as followers and disciples.

I've often looked at a couple verses from 1 Peter and thought to myself, "Wow, that is wild."

1 Peter 4:17-18

For it is time for judgment to begin at the household of God; *and if it begins with us, what will be the outcome for those who do not obey the gospel of God? And* **"If the righteous is scarcely saved,** *what will become of the ungodly and the sinner?"*

Earlier in the chapter, Peter said, "For the time that is past suffices for doing what the Gentiles want to do, living in sensuality, passions, drunkenness, orgies, drinking parties, and lawless idolatry." He goes on to make the point that we as believers don't live, or at least, shouldn't live that way and when we don't, unbelievers will persecute us. Verse 5: "With respect to this they are surprised when you do not join them in the same flood of debauchery, and they malign you." In verse 7 he says for us to be self-controlled and sober-minded. In that context, Peter goes onto say that judgment begins with the family of God, and then makes this wild statement:

And "If the righteous is scarcely saved, what will become of the ungodly and the sinner?

What does Peter mean when he says the righteous are scarcely saved? Peter, what kind of "big tent" grace talk is that?! But you see, this is exactly what Jesus meant when He talked about the narrow gate and road with few on it.

Matthew 7:13-14

Enter by the **narrow gate**. For the gate is wide and the way ("road" – NIV) is easy that leads to destruction, and those who enter by it are many. For **the gate is narrow** and the way is hard that leads to life, and those who find it are few.

"The gate is narrow and the way is hard"—not exactly a selling point for Christianity, from a human standpoint.

Many people try to see how far toward the edge of the narrow road they can walk and still be on the narrow road. They want to flirt with the very edges instead of walking on the centerline. I saw a bumper sticker one time that said, "How much sin can I get away with and still go to heaven?" That pretty much sums up the thinking of many people. The better thing to do is walk the centerline to please God with our faith and obedience. Holiness does matter.

Narrow gate, narrow road, few on it. That is reality. Let's take the aggregate of all humanity. Subtract from that number all those who don't believe that Jesus Christ was and is God and that He died on the cross for our sins or resurrected on the third day. That slims the number down quite a bit. Now take that number and subtract from that all those who profess Christ but have never truly repented, accepted and followed Jesus Christ, what we call nominal Christians (in name only). Now we're left with a very small number of people. Subtract from that number all those who are living lukewarm spiritual lives or are living in sin. Now we are left with a very, VERY small number. "If the righteous is scarcely saved" begins to make sense.

I submit to you that a healthy, reverent fear of the Lord is a critical key to living with Jesus as Lord, not just Savior. It reminds us of accountability and the judgment seat of Christ. This is a good thing. Acts 5 is the story of Ananias and his wife Sapphira lying to the Apostles. The result was that, in God's judgment, they both dropped dead, but at different times. Ananias died first, his wife Sapphira was not with him at the time (verse 1-5). After Ananias died, it says:

Acts 5:5

And great fear came upon all who heard of it.

Then in verses 7-10, later Sapphira comes in and lies to the Apostles as well. She suffered the same fate, she dropped dead as a result of God's judgment. Here's the very next verse.

Acts 5:11

And great fear came upon the whole church and upon all who heard of these things.

The reality of God's judgment on sin caused the people to have a healthy, reverent fear of God. They became aware that God is not winking at sin in the church. They found out that "judgment begins in the household of God."

Some will bristle and recoil at all of this. The typical retort is, "We are NOT to fear God. He is a compassionate and merciful God, He is all-loving." That is true. But kindness is one side of His two-fold nature—kindness and severity. Jesus Himself taught us to fear God.

Matthew 10:28

And do not fear those who kill the body but cannot kill the soul. Rather **fear him who can destroy both soul and body in hell**.

Like the contrite, humble woman with the issue of blood in Mark 5, Jesus says to those who reverence Him and need His merciful healing touch, "Do not fear, only believe," (verse 36). To those like Ananias and Sapphira who engage in sin He says, "Do not only believe, but fear." It is this reverent fear of the Lord that will cause us to do what Thomas did...fall at His feet and declare, "My Lord and my God!" (John 20:28)

Here's how the church in the book of Acts is described.

Acts 9:31

*So the church throughout all Judea and Galilee and Samaria had peace and was being built up. And **walking in the fear of the Lord and in the comfort of the Holy Spirit**, it multiplied.*

This must be a contradiction, right? It's either walking in the comfort of the Holy Spirit OR walking in the fear of the Lord, it can't be both at the same time, can it? And the answer is, yes it can. Walking in the comfort of the Holy Spirit and the fear of the Lord go hand-in-hand. Both are needed. It's the awareness of the kindness and severity of God. Savior-minded people focus on the comfort of the Holy Spirt. Lord-minded people focus on the fear of the Lord. Lord and Savior minded people enjoy a healthy balance of both.

Chapter 22

Characteristics of a Relationship

In July 1970, at the age of 17, when I first accepted Jesus Christ and began to follow Him, I attended a Young Life camp at LeTourneau Christian Center (camp & retreat center) on Canadaigua Lake, one of the finger lakes in New York State near Rochester. I stayed in a cabin with about 6-8 fellow male teenagers, and our adult cabin monitor was a guy by the name of Bill Gassett. Every night, before lights out, Bill would lead us in a little devotional. The very first night, Bill started the devotion by asking the question, "What is a Christian?" It was met with silence, and then slowly, to give the appearance that we weren't complete idiots, we began to chime in with various ideas. One said, "It's someone who goes to church, reads the Bible and prays." Bill said, "That's what a Christian does, but what is a Christian?" Another answered, "A Christian is someone who obeys Christ's commandments." Bill again responded, "That's what a Christian does, but what is a Christian?" Someone said, "Well, it's someone who worships God through Christ." Same thing, "Yes, that's what a Christian does, but what is a Christian?" It seemed like everything we said didn't fit what he was fishing for. After a while, we gave up, and then Bill began to teach us what a Christian is.

> A Christian is someone who presently is in an ongoing love relationship with God through His Son, Jesus Christ.

And although a love relationship expresses itself in doing, fundamentally, being a Christian is about a love relationship with Christ, a matter of heart devotion and affection.

Being comes before doing. The doing is an outbirth of being. Being a Christian will result in doing things, but at its root, Christianity is about **being** in a love relationship with Jesus Christ, a relationship that takes priority over all others. The being part of a love relationship is a matter of the heart (emotional connection, affections, desires), while the doing is a matter of the hand (actions). In Scripture and literature, the heart is seen as the center of one's emotions, desires and affections. It is possible to do the external doing without the heart's involvement, the being part.

Matthew 15:8

These people honor me with their lips, but their hearts are far from me. (NIV)

As with any love relationship, there are indications or telltale signs that indicate and affirm that there truly is a serious, committed relationship going on.

When atheists or others come against the validity of Christianity they, sooner or later, bring up the crusades (1100-1200 AD) and make the charge, "This is what religion has done, this is what Christians have done, that is what Christianity is." Certainly during the crusades, there was a small segment of that group that raped, murdered innocents and pillaged people and property. But it's important to note that those who murdered or raped weren't Christians, because true Christians would never act like that. Jesus was very clear and stated that people who claim to be His but act contrary to Him, aren't Christians. "Not everyone who says to me, 'Lord, Lord,' will enter the kingdom of heaven, but only the one who does the will of my Father who is in heaven." (Matthew 7:21 - NIV). Notice the word "does". The *doing* doesn't get people into heaven, but doing does become a telltale sign or indicator, proof if you will, that a person truly is living in a relationship with Christ as Lord.

And just because someone attends a Christian church doesn't mean they are a Christian. Churches are full of people who aren't Christians. Back to Bill Gassett's question, what is a Christian?

It's been said that Christianity is not a religion, but a relationship. I like that, I believe that's the key to understanding what a Christian is. I believe it's the key to understanding what discipleship is, which is the process of growing spiritually. Understanding what a Christian is by seeing it through the lens of a love relationship is crucial to the premise of this entire book. Love and commitment are first of all internal, eventually expressing itself in conduct.

What is a Christian? A Christian is someone who is a committed follower of Jesus Christ and experiences an ongoing, vibrant and developing love relationship with Him.

If Christianity is primarily a relationship, that got me thinking about characteristics of a committed relationship, say in a marriage. That's not a bad analogy, even the Apostle Paul looked at it that way.

Ephesians 5:24-25

Now as the church submits to Christ, so also wives should submit to their husbands in everything. Husbands, love your wives, just as Christ loved the church and gave himself up for her. (NIV)

The husband-wife relationship is compared to the Christ-church relationship. In both cases, it's all about relationship, a committed, close, and vibrant love relationship.

In the 2016 presidential election both political candidates claimed to be a "Christian". Other candidates before the contenders were whittled down all claimed to be Christians as well (with the exception of one Jewish candidate). I mean, how is one to tell? One could list famous musical artists that claim to be Christian but whose lyrics and behavior are ungodly. Just like the crusades, there are a lot of "posers" out there.

So how do you tell? Well, Jesus didn't leave us wondering. Jesus said "by their fruit you will recognize them." (Matthew 7:15-20) Bad tree, bad fruit; good tree, good fruit. It should be noted that what determines good and bad fruit is the **relationship** it has to the tree. An intrinsic relationship to a good tree produces one thing, while an intrinsic relationship to a bad tree produces another. It's all about relationship. I don't see this as much different than a marriage. A fundamentally good marital relationship produces harmony, understanding, love and intimacy, while a fundamentally bad marital relationship produces division, bitterness, suspicion and discord. It's all about the quality of the relationship, which in turn produces fruit or results.

As I have meditated and pondered this whole relationship thing as it relates to the question of "What is a Christian?", I've distilled it down to eight things. It could contain a lot more, but they would all be variants of these eight elements. What is a Christian? A Christian is someone who has a vibrant, ongoing, developing love relationship with Jesus Christ as nurtured and expressed by these characteristics.

EIGHT CHARACTERISTICS OF RELATIONSHIP

1. Passion/affection.
2. Intimacy through quantity/quality time.
3. Communication.
4. Exclusivity.
5. Pleasing behavior.
6. Giving.
7. Serving.
8. Telling others.

Let me touch on each briefly.

1. Passion

Passion is strong desire. When an engaged couple or a husband and wife are truly in love, each has passion, a strong desire, a yearning as it were, to be with their partner. They yearn to be with them, to love them, to hang out together. When apart they miss each other and can't wait to be with each other again.

The same is true with our relationship with Jesus Christ. A genuine Christian or disciple has passion about their relationship with the Lord. They yearn to love, serve, increase their knowledge of, and worship God

Psalm 42:1-2

As a deer pants for flowing streams, so pants my soul for you, O God. My soul thirsts for God, for the living God.

Passion or strong desire is manifested through the other elements in this chapter. A lack of passion for God indicates a problem, and may even indicate the person is not a disciple of Jesus Christ. Are our hearts pulled toward God? Do our affections and desires center in Christ?

Colossians 3:1-2

Since, then, you have been raised with Christ, set your hearts on things above, where Christ is, seated at the right hand of God. Set your minds on things above, not on earthly things. (NIV)

Here we see the primary indicator of a relationship ... affections and desires of the heart.

2. Intimacy through quantity/quality time

Here we mean both quantity AND quality time together. It's possible for a husband and wife to be together but not have communication or intimacy. Their attention and minds are in different places. This verse bears repeating.

Matthew 15:8

These people honor me with their lips, but their hearts are far from me. (NIV)

There are times that I've spent twenty-five minutes in worship and probably only ten minutes of that was when I was truly "present" in worship with my whole being. Numerous times I've read five to ten chapters of Scripture and when done, the Holy Spirit would whisper inside of me, "What did you read, what was it all about and how does it apply to your life?", and I would reply, "I don't know." I was reading God's Word on autopilot with my mind on other things.

How does a disciple spend quantity and quality time with the Lord? Primarily it comes down to these four things:

1. Worship
2. Prayer (including conversational and listening prayer)
3. Reading and studying God's Word
4. Meditation

When we worship God, we acknowledge our submission and acknowledgment of Him as the Lord of our lives. Regular, deep and genuine worship creates intimacy with God and strengthens our relationship with Him.

John 4:23

*But the hour is coming, and is now here, when the true worshipers will **worship the Father in spirit and truth**, for the Father is seeking such people to worship him.*

Worship and prayer are essential ways of strengthening our relationship with the Lord. I'll touch on prayer shortly. If someone claims to be a Christian, a disciple, but they don't spend time with God through worship and prayer, I would question the genuineness of that relationship in the very same way I would question a husband who claims to have a wonderful relationship with His wife, but never spends quantity and quality time with her.

In a love relationship, it's important to spend time for the purpose of getting to know that person intimately. Time spent (or really, invested) with someone results in progressively more understanding and knowledge of that person. That's why a lot of quick engagements don't work, because they haven't spent enough quantity and quality time with each other and consequently don't have sufficient knowledge of that person.

1 Peter 3:7

Likewise, husbands, live with your wives in an understanding way (KJV – according to knowledge).

So one key to relationship is quantity/quality time for the express purpose of getting to know that person, growing in intimate, experiential knowledge and understanding of them. The same is true in our relationship with the Lord.

Almost all of us intimately know authors we've never met simply through voracious reading of their works. I don't know Bill Hybels or Rick Warren personally, but boy, do I know them! I've read their stuff and I know what they believe, how they think and could even predict how they'd act or make decisions in a certain situation. Someone that's having a true, genuine relationship with God is going to know God through His Word.

Psalm 119:16, 24

I delight in your decrees; I will not neglect your word. — Your statutes are my delight; they are my counselors." (NIV)

Reading God's Word on a daily basis is the way we spend time with God and get to know Him. A true, genuine relationship will result in intentional carving out of time to spend with them. When I was first dating my wife Debby, because we both were in Bible school, we didn't see each other much, except for sharing the last class of the day together. After school we both worked jobs and couldn't see each other then, or in evenings because I worked until midnight. But you better believe that I was very intentional about carving out time on the weekends to be with her. It was a priority. A Christian values time with God through His Word.

Job 23:12

I have not departed from the commandment of his lips; I have treasured the words of his mouth more than my portion of food.

Jeremiah 15:16

Your words were found, and I ate them, and your words became to me a joy and the delight of my heart,

People who claim to be Christians but don't read and study God's Word, at the very least, are showing they don't understand what it means to be a Christian, which I remind you, is a relationship, and relationships are based on time spent with each other. Wouldn't you, in your own mind, question someone who claimed to have an intimate, deep and great relationship with their spouse but then you found out they never spent quantity/quality time with them? It would be a contradiction. Behavior is fruit that locates a person.

This touches on the ancient Jewish meaning of an apprentice following a rabbi. When someone was asked to follow a rabbi, it meant reordering their entire life to follow, walk, talk, study, spend time with and learn from the rabbi. Their time was not their own anymore. Following the rabbi became the #1 priority. Jesus was called "Rabbi" sixteen times in the gospels. And Jesus, when calling His disciples, invited them by saying, "Follow Me." In all cases, this meant dropping what they were doing and from that moment on, putting time spent with Jesus as their #1 priority.

Relationship is developed and nurtured by spending quantity/quality time with that person. It's true for your spouse, it's true for Jesus. With Christians, spending time with God, getting

211

to know Him on a deep level, is done through reading and studying His Word.

Philippians 3:10

And this, so that I may know Him [experientially, becoming more thoroughly acquainted with Him, understanding the remarkable wonders of His Person more completely] and [in that same way experience] the power of His resurrection [which overflows and is active in believers]. (Amplified Bible)

Philippians 3:8

*Yes, everything else is worthless when compared with the infinite value of knowing Christ Jesus my **Lord**. For his sake I have discarded everything else, counting it all as garbage, so that I could gain Christ. (NLT)*

Christianity, discipleship, is making knowing Christ a priority, and we know Christ by reading and studying God's Word.

This would also include meditating on God's Word. Meditation is when we slow down, get quiet and think and muse deeply about God and His Word. We stop and ponder it deeply...chewing it over in our minds.

Joshua 1:8

This Book of the Law shall not depart from your mouth, but you shall meditate on it day and night, so that you may be careful to do according to all that is written in it. For then you will make your way prosperous, and then you will have good success.

Psalm 63:5-6

My mouth will praise you with joyful lips, when I remember you upon my bed, and meditate on you in the watches of the night.

3. Communication

A genuine relationship is both defined and expressed by intentional ongoing and deep communication. In our relationship with Christ, this means prayer, both speaking and listening prayer. I would question and certainly wonder about someone who claimed to be a Christian yet seldom prayed. That action, or lack of action, would be evidence of a heart disconnect in the relationship. A committed relationship of the heart will always result in both the desire and the action of frequent and deep communication.

We see this in the life of Jesus Himself in His relationship with His Father.

Luke 5:16

But Jesus often withdrew to lonely places and prayed.

Mark 1:35

And rising very early in the morning, while it was still dark, he departed and went out to a desolate place, and there he prayed.

Jesus had an intimate relationship with His Father that was fueled, energized and nurtured through prayer. This includes both speaking prayer (petition) and listening prayer, when we become quiet before God and just sense what He is saying to us.

Psalm 46:10

Be still, and know that I am God.

John 10:27

***My sheep listen** to my voice; I know them, and they follow me. (NIV)*

An active, vibrant prayer life is one of the marks of a true Christian who is in a committed, love relationship with Jesus Christ.

4. Exclusivity.

An important characteristic of a committed love relationship is exclusivity—that person, the one you're married to, becomes the most important person in your life. You will highly esteem that relationship above all others and will not allow another to take their place.

For a true disciple or Christian, Jesus Christ must be the most important person in their life. This is exactly what Jesus meant in Luke 14.

Luke 14:26

If anyone comes to me and does not hate his own father and mother and wife and children and brothers and sisters, yes, and even his own life, he cannot be my disciple.

We should interpret "hate" as "love less in comparison to." For example, here's how Matthew's account reads:

Matthew 10:27

*Whoever loves father or mother **more than me** is not worthy of me, and whoever loves son or daughter **more than me** is not worthy of me.*

"More than" is the key here. If one loves their spouse or child *more than* Jesus Christ, they are not a disciple of Jesus Christ. Jesus Christ must be the top priority relationship in one's life, with NO close second places.

Colossians 1:8

That in everything he might be preeminent.

One of the marks of a true disciple is exclusivity...allowing no person, thing or pursuit to take the place of Christ.

1 John 5:21

*Little children, **keep yourselves from idols**.*

And this was written to Christians!

5. Pleasing behavior.

When one is in a committed love relationship with another, they want to engage in behaviors that please their spouse. Desiring to please the one we love is a natural outbirth of love.

I remember reading a book by Larry Halter that was first published in 1988 called, *Traits of a Happy Couple*. The book is out of print, although copies can still be obtained on Amazon, Barnes and Noble and other outlets. I wish it wasn't out of print because I found it very helpful. The author talked about traits of happy couples compared with those of unhappy couples. The author examined twelve happy couples and twelve unhappy couples. He found that happy couples have a ratio of *pleasing behaviors* to *unpleasing behaviors* of 17:1. For every one unpleasing or negative behavior, they had seventeen positive partner-pleasing behaviors. Unhappy couples only had a ratio of 3:1. The point here is—love engages in pleasing behavior toward the one loved, and for disciples, that means:

- Faith
- Obedience
- Holiness.

This is how we please God.

Hebrews 11:6

*And **without faith it is impossible to please him**, for whoever would draw near to God must believe that he exists and that he rewards those who seek him.*

1 Samuel 15:22

*Has the Lord as great delight in burnt offerings and sacrifices, as in **obeying** the voice of the Lord? Behold, to **obey** is better than sacrifice*

1 John 3:22

*Whatever we ask we receive from him, because **we keep his commandments** and **do what pleases him**.*

1 Thessalonians 4:1,3,7

*Finally, then, brothers, we ask and urge you in the Lord Jesus, that as you received from us **how you ought to walk and to please God**, just as you are doing, that you do so more and*

*more. ... For this is the will of God, **your sanctification**. ...
For God has not called us for impurity, but in **holiness**.*

We please God through faith, obedience and holiness. They are characteristics of someone who is in a love relationship with Christ. The absence of faith, obedience and holiness indicate that something is wrong in the relationship and even that the relationship may be in peril.

6. Giving.

John 3:16

***For God so loved the world, that he gave** his only Son, that whoever believes in him should not perish but have eternal life.*

God so loved the world that He gave. Giving is an expression of love, both in a love relationship with our spouse as well as with God. With giving, for the most part, we mean giving in three areas: time, talent and treasure. With time and talent, are we regularly volunteering in the local church and Kingdom of God in general using our spiritual gifts? Regarding treasure, do we honor God with our tithes and offerings regularly? Financial giving to the Kingdom of God is a significant mark of a disciple. One can give and not be a disciple, but you can't be a true disciple without being a giver. Jesus warned about this.

Matthew 6:24

*No one can serve two masters, for either he will hate the one and love the other, or he will be devoted to the one and despise the other. **You cannot serve God and money**.*

We see the connection between love and giving in a passage from 2 Corinthians 8. The subject in the chapter is financial giving.

2 Corinthians 8:7-8

*But as you excel in everything—in faith, in speech, in knowledge, in all earnestness, and in our love for you—**see that you excel in this act of grace** (the act of giving) also. I say this not as a command, but to **prove by the earnestness of others that your love also is genuine**.*

Giving is an outbirth of love. If someone does not regularly give tithes and offerings to God, it's either because they haven't been taught or because money has become an idol, taking the place of God.

7. Serving.

One of the marks of a true disciple of Jesus Christ is servanthood. Because I covered this in detail in Chapter 19, *Son or Servant?*, I won't take much time to cover it now. The questions here are: *Am I serving the Lord on a regular basis using my spiritual gifts? Am I serving the Lord on a regular basis by serving Him through serving others?* We weren't saved to sit, we were saved to serve.

Hebrews 9:14

> *How much more will the blood of Christ, who through the eternal Spirit offered himself without blemish to God, purify our conscience from dead works **to serve the living God**.*

Ephesians 2:8, 10

> *For by grace you have been saved through faith. ... For we are his workmanship, **created in Christ Jesus for good works**, which God prepared beforehand, that we should walk in them.*

Now that we've been saved, we're to serve the living God. Typically someone will respond, "Well, I serve God and others through my job and career." You may, but that's not what we're talking about here. Let's discount for now activities that make us money because the line between serving others and serving ourselves becomes blurred.

Those who love God, serve Him and others.

Titus 3:8

> *That those who have believed in God may be careful to **devote themselves to good works**. These things are excellent and profitable for people.*

One big way we serve God is by our next point.

8. Telling others.

A significant aspect of being a disciple of Jesus Christ is sharing the Good News with other people. If Christ is the most important relationship in the whole world to us, why would we be silent or incognito about this? If Christ is the most important thing in our life, would we not share that with others? What would you think of someone whom you had closely worked with for the last year and then just found out that he or she had gotten engaged six months ago, and that their fiancé was the most important thing in their life, and that their whole life is oriented around their fiancé ... but they never told you? You would correctly deduce one of two things?

1. They're not really telling the truth. Their fiancé and engagement is not really that important to them. Or ...

2. You're not that important to them.

Either option is troubling. If we do not share Christ with other people, either Christ is not that important to us, OR ... the people we come in contact with are not that important to us. Yet, we are commanded to share the Good News (the gospel) with other people.

Matthew 28:19-20

Go therefore and make disciples of all nations, baptizing them in the name of the Father and of the Son and of the Holy Spirit, teaching them to observe all that I have commanded you.

This is not a suggestion, it is a command. And it's a command to all of us, not just extroverts. Jesus taught that true followers make their mission to reach out to people far from God with the gospel of salvation.

Matthew 4:19

Follow me, and I will make you fishers of men.

The converse is true as well—those of His followers who aren't fishers of men aren't fully following Him. That can and should change.

Keep in mind that all of us are accountable before God to share Christ with others, but God works in line or in harmony with our personalities. Not all of us are going to be as bold as others just because of our temperaments. I encourage you to read the book, *Becoming a Contagious Christian*, by Bill Hybels and Mark Mittelberg, to learn your particular evangelistic style.[21] There are six of them: confrontational (or direct) style, intellectual style, testimonial style, interpersonal style, invitational style, and serving style.

The point here, is that one important characteristic of a true disciple of Christ or Christian, is that they share Christ with others when the opportunity arises. Never or seldom sharing Christ with others indicates a problem in the relationship.

Remember the injunction to us from the Apostle Paul in 2 Corinthians 13:5

2 Corinthians 13:5

Examine yourselves, to see whether you are in the faith. Test yourselves. Or do you not realize this about yourselves, that Jesus Christ is in you?—unless indeed you fail to meet the test!

Ask yourselves these questions to help with the test.

1. Do I possess a strong passion and affection for Jesus Christ and following Him?
2. Do I spend both quantity and quality time with the Lord through worship, prayer, bible reading and meditation?
3. Do I spend daily time with God in prayer, both speaking (petition) and listening?
4. Does my life reflect that my relationship with Jesus Christ is the most important thing in my life?
5. Do I regularly engage in pleasing behavior toward the Lord, through continuing faith, obedience and holiness?
6. Do I give financially in a significant way to the local church and the Kingdom of God?

---

21 Becoming a Contagious Christian, Bill Hybels and Mark Mittelberg, 1996, Zondervan

7. Do I serve the Lord through the local church and Kingdom of God by using my spiritual gifts?
8. Do I share the Good News of salvation through Jesus Christ with others when the opportunity arises?

Are the majority of these eight characteristics evident in your life?

Chapter 23

Grace for Enduring

The case being made in this book is that Jesus Christ is not only a Savior to be received from, but our Lord to be obeyed and faithfully followed. Receiving Christ at an altar call X years ago is a start, but the Lord is interested in those who finish. It's about endurance.

Matthew 24:13

*But the one who **endures to the end will be saved**.*

Only the ones who stay faithful and endure to the end will be saved. Eternal life is about presently having a vital relationship with Jesus Christ, not having it one time in the past.

1 John 5:11-12

*God gave us eternal life, and this life is in his Son. Whoever **has** the Son has life; whoever **does not have** the Son of God does not have life.*

"Has" is present tense and means "to hold." It's the same Greek word used in the case of the rich young ruler who walked away from Jesus.

Mark 10:22

*Disheartened by the saying, he went away sorrowful, for he **had** (presently, at that moment) great possessions.*

The rich young ruler presently "had" and was "holding onto" his wealth and possessions. Whoever **has** and **holds onto** the Son has eternal life. This is talking about having/holding onto the Son in a vital, living way—an ongoing vital relationship. The word "vital" means, "existing as a manifestation of life."[22] A *vital* relationship is one in which there is an observable manifestation of real life. Only those who continue to believe and follow the Son, have the Son.

This certainly doesn't mean perfection. It doesn't mean a sinless life. None of us will ever attain that on this side of heaven, although it should be our goal (Matthew 5:48). But it does mean faithfully following Jesus Christ as Lord, Master, Owner and Supreme in Authority in our lives.

Lest we think that the efficacy of endurance is based solely on self-will and fleshly efforts, we must stress that endurance is achieved by cooperation between our will and the power of the Spirit. It isn't all the Spirit, and it isn't all on our will and effort. Endurance is empowered by the Holy Spirit as we yield and surrender to His power, even in our weakness.

2 Corinthians 12:10

For when I am weak, then I am strong.

The Apostle Paul lets shows us the key to all of this in Galatians 2.

Galatians 2:20

*I have been crucified with Christ. **It is no longer I who live, but Christ who lives in me.** And the life I now live in the flesh I live by faith in the Son of God, who loved me and gave himself for me.*

Paul came to experience the power of Christ living in and through him through faith. He lived a life in the flesh, but empowered by the power of God. The keys are surrender and trust.

2 Corinthians 4:7

*But we have this treasure in jars of clay, to show that **the surpassing power belongs to God and not to us.***

---

[22] Vital - https://www.merriam-webster.com/dictionary/vital

Ephesians 1:19

*What is **the immeasurable greatness of his power toward us who believe**, according to the working of his great might.*

We have access to immeasurable power to help us on our spiritual journey. We need to be diligently appropriating that power to help us endure while we *fight the good fight* (2 Timothy 4:4). But there is the human side to enduring that we should not slight or neglect. Just like 2 Corinthians 4:7 (we have this treasure in jars of clay), there is another passage that talks about earthen vessels that we must not ignore.

2 Timothy 2:20-21

*Now in a great house there are not only vessels of gold and silver but also of wood and clay, some for honorable use, some for dishonorable. Therefore, **if anyone cleanses himself** from what is dishonorable, he will be a vessel for honorable use, set apart as holy, useful to the master of the house, ready for every good work.*

"If anyone cleanses himself." This is very much like 1 John 3:3.

1 John 3:3

*And everyone who thus hopes in him **purifies himself** as he is pure.*

That denotes responsibility and effort on the part of the individual. The balance to all this that there is a God part and a human part. I'll touch on more detail of the human part shortly. Our part is to give God **permission** to show His **power** on our behalf as we look to Him in faith and trust Him. This is the **permission/power principle**...our permission (surrender) and His power (enabling us to endure). I believe this is what Jesus meant in Matthew 26:41.

Matthew 26:41

Watch and pray that you may not enter into temptation. The spirit indeed is willing, but the flesh is weak.

What's implicit here is that when we pray, we ask God for help, we give Him permission to break into our lives with supernatural assistance, and...He will. Jesus taught us to pray this way.

Matthew 6:13

And lead us not into temptation, but deliver us from evil.

Pray, invite God into your situation, give Him permission to help you become victorious in the midst of temptation through His power. Again, it is the **permission/power principle**, and it is one of two keys to endurance (I'll touch on the other shortly). To endure, we must look to Him.

Hebrews 12:1-2

*Let us run with endurance the race that is set before us, **looking to Jesus**.*

"Looking to Jesus" is the key to endurance. It means seeking Him first above all things, and actively asking Him for the power to endure. That power comes to us through God's grace.

2 Corinthians 6:1

***Working together with him**, then, we appeal to you not to receive the grace of God in vain.*

It's not all God, it's not all us—it's working together with Him through grace.

2 Thessalonians 3:5

*May the Lord direct your hearts to the love of God and to **the steadfastness of Christ**.*

As our focus and attention is directed Godward, we experience "the steadfastness of Christ."

But there is another aspect to enduring in grace that needs mentioning. This is the part we play.

ENDURANCE AND TRAINING

Just as endurance is tied to training for athletes, so endurance is tied to training for our spiritual journey. John Ortberg, in his book *The Life You've Always Wanted*, does an excellent job explaining this.[23] I'll paraphrase. We can only do through *training* what we cannot do through *trying*. For most of us, we couldn't run a 26.2-mile marathon in under four hours, even if we tried real hard. But what if, for a year or two, you reoriented your entire life around training; including a coach, strict nutrition and rest, regimented training, measured progress with goals and varied long-distance running climates and situations. In time, you eventually could run that marathon in under four hours. The success in endurance wasn't based on *trying*, it was based on *training*.

Spiritual success and endurance works the same way, except that we call the various exercises, *spiritual disciplines.*

1 Timothy 4:7-8

Train yourself for godliness; *for while bodily training is of some value, godliness is of value in every way, as it holds promise for the present life and also for the life to come.*

Spiritual training for godliness (holiness) involves exercises or disciplines that we choose to do on a regular basis. When we take the time to engage in these various spiritual disciplines, we experience motivation, a transformed mind, strength, endurance and success as followers of Christ. But it starts with passion and affection for following God closely.

Psalm 63:8

My soul clings to you; your right hand upholds me.

The Holman Christian Standard Bible reads,

I follow close to You.

---

[23]   John Ortberg, *The Life You've Always Wanted*, Reprint 2015, Zondervan

I still like the King James Version for this verse:

My soul followeth hard after thee.

How does one follow hard after God? How do we cling to the Lord in a vital relationship? We engage in the very things (disciplines and exercises) we talked about in Chapter 22, *Characteristics of a Relationship*:

1. Passion
2. Intimacy through quantity/quality time
   - Worship
   - Bible reading and study
   - Prayer
   - Meditation
3. Communication.
4. Exclusivity.
5. Pleasing behavior.
   - Faith
   - Obedience
   - Holiness
6. Giving.
7. Serving.
8. Telling others.

This spiritual training produces endurance. The God part of the equation is His power as we give Him permission to help us (*the immeasurable greatness of his power toward us who believe –* Ephesians 1:19). Our part is to engage in these spiritual exercises. It's not all God and it's not all us. No angel is going to appear and take you by the hand, leading you to the place of bible study or prayer. It takes a decision coupled with follow-through.

Another aspect of success in enduring is staying closely and regularly connected to people who themselves are *following hard after God*. They will encourage you to stay faithful to the Lord.

Hebrews 10:24-25

*And let us consider how to **stir up one another** to love and good works, **not neglecting to meet together**, as is the habit of some, but encouraging one another, and all the more as you see the Day drawing near.*

We're called to "stir up one another to love and good works." The NIV says, *spur one another on.* The NLT says, *motivate one another.* When we regularly get around other Christ-followers, we become more motivated to *follow hard after God.* Accountability is a good thing.

PUTTING IT ALL TOGETHER

The purpose of this book is to help us understand that Jesus Christ is Lord and Savior...a Savior to be received from, certainly, but also a Lord to be obeyed and followed. It is my contention that much of the Body of Christ is not fully aware of this. So in closing, let me summarize by giving you the main points covered in this book.

1.   Many people who *profess* Christ, don't *possess* Christ, and therefore will not experience eternal life.

2.   Being born again involves: repent, believe, receive and follow.

3.   A faith that does not have corresponding works of obedience is a dead faith.

4.   Salvation is a process involving the past, present and future.

5.   Assurance of salvation is not a prayer said X number of years ago, but continued faithfulness in following Christ.

6.   We can test ourselves to see if we're truly in the faith by looking at evidence.

7.   We will recognize genuine disciples of Jesus Christ by their fruit, that is, their behavior and conduct... their *walk*, not just by their *talk*.

8.   Jesus Christ is both a Savior to be received from and a Lord to be obeyed. Many people who accept Christ as *Savior*, to rescue them from their sins and hell, have not truly bowed their knee to Him as *Lord*.

9. It is possible for someone to forfeit their salvation and eternal life, by four things:
   - Intentional rejection of Jesus Christ
   - A continued willful lifestyle of sin
   - Living a lukewarm lifestyle
   - Embracing heresy

10. We are both *sons* and *slaves* of God.

11. What is needed in the Body of Christ is a healthy, reverent fear of the Lord.

12. Christianity is a relationship, and the evidence for a relationship with Christ is similar to the characteristics of a love relationship between a husband and wife.

13. God, in His grace, gives strength and power for us to endure and faithfully follow Him. At the same time, there are spiritual exercises that we can engage in that will help us to endure and stay faithful to Jesus as both Lord and Savior.

May the Lord awaken all of us to the need to walk with Jesus Christ as both Lord and Savior. He truly is a Savior to be received from. We are so grateful for that. But He is also a Lord to be obeyed. May we, like Thomas, fall at His feet and cry, "My Lord and my God!"

ABOUT THE AUTHOR

Tom Peers has been in ministry since 1979. He grew up in Brockport, New York; attended Monroe Community College, Rochester, New York; State University of New York at Brockport, served in the United States Air Force and Air National Guard, graduated from Rhema Bible College in Broken Arrow, Oklahoma, and attended Elim Bible Institute, Lima, New York.

Tom has served as a pastor in Rochester, New York; Lake Worth, Florida; Florence, Kentucky; Cumberland, Maine and Portsmouth, New Hampshire; along with serving as Director of Operations for a Christian ministry in Phoenix, Arizona. He has also served fulltime as a certified church consultant. Tom and his wife Debby have two children, Jesse and Carissa, each with families of their own. Tom and Debby currently reside in Portland, Maine.

tompeers53@gmail.com

Books by Tom Peers:

The Pastor and the Prayer
Addiction Recovery Through Living the Serenity Prayer

Lord and Savior
A Savior to be Received From – A Lord to be Obeyed

Fit, Function and Flourish
Your Place and Function in the Local Church

Is God to Blame?
Reconciling Suffering with a Good God

How to Be a Prime Target
We're All Targets – Some Make Better Targets Than Others

Mixed Nuts
Brain Droppings From a Retired Pastor

www.ingramcontent.com/pod-product-compliance
Lightning Source LLC
Chambersburg PA
CBHW070952040426
42443CB00007B/480